Falling for a Thugstress

Chicago   Pentress

DEDICATION

I will like to dedicate my book to my mom Gwen, my Aunt Nita, my brothers Milton aka Chubb, Mark, and Damien aka Damo, my eight kids, Ja'Von, Da'Naiya, De' Asia, Jamaria, Lil Rob, Javontae, Baby May May, and Samya, my supporters, and last but not least, my partna in crime Rob, I love you, baby.

Thank you all for being there for me through it all and standing by my side and to my eight kids, I want y'all to remember that the sky is the limit. Love you all to the max.

I would like to express my gratitude to the many people who saw me through this book; to all those who provided support, talked things over, read, and offered comments.

I will like to thank God for being the head of my life and giving me the talent to be a writer!

I will like to thank Shavonne for sharing my story on her Facebook page. Because of you, my book was able to reach people nationwide. I also want to thank all my supporters for motivating me and getting me through those days when I didn't feel like pushing through.

Special thanks go to Sheree aka Ree Babi. I gained you as a friend and that alone means the world to me. Tacarra, I didn't forget you. You're the best. To anybody else that I forgot to mention, charge it to my head and not my heart. Free my brother, Damo. Sleep peacefully, Jamario. I love and miss you.

.

ACKNOWLEDGMENTS

Thank you, Damien, for making my book cover. I love you, bro.
.

chapter one

Keisha woke up feeling on top of the world. This nigga just put it on me. The dick was so good that it got a bitch making breakfast. Wait until I tell Choc how I got that nigga, Smoke, last night. She's gonna be so fuckin' mad.

Choc is one of those goofy bitches, she always fuckin' with these niggas that be sellin' packs for the big hitters. Me on the other hand, I only deal with the bossed-up niggas with that never-ending Warren Buffet money. I be trying to tell Choc's dumb ass to stop fuckin' with these broke ass niggas, but she's a weak-minded, silly bitch out here fuckin' to get her motherfuckin' rent paid. A bad bitch like me be wettin' this ass for ownership, shares, and chinchillas.

Smoke was a boss nigga in the streets. He had the whole South Side on lock, and on top of that, every bitch wanted him. His dick was big and long just like his pockets. "I rode that nigga's dick so good," Keisha thought to herself while in the kitchen fixing Smoke's plate. He busted all inside of this little tight pussy and told me my kitty cat was better than any bitch he's ever had. This nigga thinks he's tellin' me what I want to hear. However, what he doesn't know is that I got somethin' planned for him and his pockets. I'm young, but not dumb. Money makes me cum. Let me go feed this trick, so he can get the fuck up outta my crib.

Keisha walked into the room Smoke was stretched out on her king size bed looking sexy with his long dreads and chocolate skin. He was smoking his loud and talking on his phone when Keisha entered the

1

room. Smoke waved his hand for Keisha to come service him but little did she know that this nigga had some tricks up his sleeve too. Smoke never told Keisha about his other woman Lady Luck she's one ruthless ass bitch and will fuck a hoe up about Smoke's ass.

Let me call this bitch, Choc. Keisha grabbed her phone off the nightstand and dialed Choc's number. Choc picked up on the first ring. "Hoe, you'll never believe what I've been doing and who I've been doing it with!"

Choc looked at her phone unimpressed. "Bitch who? Not that I care because you're always with somebodies' man." Choc and Keisha were both nineteen years old. Choc was short and thick, small waist, big round ass with small breast. She wasn't good looking like Keisha, Choc just had a nice body. She was from the city's low-end she didn't have a perfect life, being sat out by her crack whore mama and fucked by her dad continuously, so loyalty to a friend was the last thing on her mind. "Bitch, did you wake up on the wrong side of the bed or are you mad because you weren't gettin' dick down by somebody's man last night?" I asked, jokingly.

"Mad for what? Bitch, please!" Choc answered with an angry tone.

"Yea, you're mad like always," Keisha replied sarcastically. "Anyway bitch, I was gettin' it in with that nigga, Smoke, last night. The brother had me climbing walls, making breakfast and all that good shit. I sucked his dick so good that he left me a little shopping money for tonight. You wanna go grab some fits to dance in for the party? You know the tricks are gonna be out spending that cash and I know I wanna be lookin' good."

"Hell yea, bitch!" Choc yelled through the phone.

"Okay girl, I'll see you around three and be ready."

"Okay, bye." Choc hung up the phone.

"This is one thirsty ass bitch!" Keisha murmured to herself while staring at her phone. "Hoes be happy as hell when I come up off these niggas, but be mad when I'm fuckin' these niggas. Let me hop in this shower."

"Keisha always gets the good ones," Choc thought to herself. It's cool though. I have something planned for her ass. I can't keep letting this bitch shit on me. I feel like she does that shit just to rub it in my face. Keisha has always had more than I have. She didn't have to go through the shit I went through with my mom and dad. Despite the fact that her parents were about that street life and were in and out of jail, she still manages to think with a clear head and get that money. I hate that about her," Choc spoke aloud to herself.

The number one rule is to keep your friends close and your enemies closer. That's the rule I live by. I know that this slut ain't gonna call or come through, so let me get dressed and go to this club by my damn self. That bitch is dead to me!

Lady Luck was driving up 63rd Street with Young Thug's "Stoner" blaring from the speakers in her new 2016 Monte Carlo SS. Smoke just purchased her the nice whip for being a down ass bitch. Lady Luck is a bad bitch that didn't take any shit from anybody. She was on her way to the Red Diamond Strip Club wearing a custom-made catsuit with 6-inch Red Bottoms with diamonds on the bottom of the shoe. Her hair was in a long, sleek, twenty-inch ponytail that dropped to her ass.

Lady Luck stood five-foot-six with a body of a goddess. Her chocolate skin was smooth like butter and she had hazel cat eyes to die for, and nails that were naturally long and manicured. I can't wait to shut this party down. I can't wait until Smoke sees me. He's going to regret that he chose to stay out all night.

Pulling up at the club, the parking lot was lit. You would've thought that the party was outside because niggas and their women were hand and hand. The trap boys were out tonight and some of everybody's baby mamas too.

"Damn, this bitch is packed with hoes and balling ass niggas. Where is my Smoke?" Lady Luck looked in the crowd and couldn't spot her man for shit. "I know his ass up here and he better not be with a thot ass bitch because I will show my ass in the worst way. This nigga already knows I'm not to be played with from what happen to the last bitch he was caught cheating on me with." She was found dead in the alley with her throat slit... She continued on trying to spot Smoke while talking herself down from spazzing.

Yes, I'm about to get it in tonight. I just got this rental and I can't wait to slide in this all white thang. I heard Red Diamond is cracking already with all those boss ass niggas. I'm trying to fuck Smoke tonight though, so I can't go way out like I normally would. Shit, let me go pick up my friend Nicole. It's already ten on the dot. I was about to go get Choc, but I'm not feeling her phony ass energy like that. She's been acting really different lately. That bitch is up to something, I just don't know what it is. Nicole has been my best friends for years. She's a bad bitch like me and I know that I can trust her. She has never done shit to make me question her loyalty. I pulled up to Nicole's house where she lived with her mama.

We're about to shut this club down, Keisha thought to herself.

"Nicole, you ready?" Keisha asked as she walked in the door.

"Yea bitch, come on. I'm ready to blow this loud and get to it," Nicole happily sang. They got in the car and sped off into traffic heading towards the club.

"Nicole, I don't know if I'm feeling that motherfucking Choc bitch; it's just something about her. She's becoming a hater, every single day it's something new with her," Keisha tried to explain how she felt.

"Well, bitch let me kill her." They both started laughing. "I'm serious Nicole, something is up with her. She be jealous every time I fuck with a nigga with some money but she always got her hands out I'm tired of looking out for her when she never brings shit to the table but fingertips and lips. "Bitch, you already know what you got to do. It ain't shit to cut that bitch off."

This bitch thinks it's a game, huh? This hoe is trying to play me. That bitch didn't even call me, that's why I left and did my own thing. I tell you about these goofy ass hoes, one minute they love you and the next minute they hate you. That's why I always kept my guard up with the bitch anyway. I'm so ready to erase that bitch it ain't even funny. That's why every nigga she fucked, I sucked they dick right after and Smoke, I'm going to give him every piece of me too. The phone ringing startled Choc from her thoughts. She picked up without looking at the caller ID. "What's up?" Choc said.

"Hey bitch, are you meeting me at the club or nah? I'm ready to shake my ass for some cash."

"Keisha, you're a phony ass bitch! I'm already here. Don't fucking call me, hoe," and she hung up in Keisha's face. Keisha looked at her phone thinking, "I know this goofy, ugly ass bitch didn't just hang up on me. I got something for this scum ass bitch."

Smoke was sitting in the VIP section with a lot of thick pretty bitches, dancing all over him he had some of his homies there with him. Smoke ordered Cîroc and patron for the V.I.P. Section. He had a stack of cash sitting on his lap with a loud blunt hanging from his lips smoke was dripped in diamonds he had a long Jesus piece around his neck his

Marc Jacob fully iced out stainless steel watch was shining from all the diamonds.

Smoke wore an all-white Polo jogging suit, a white snapback hat with his name across the front in diamonds. Bitches knew when Smoke came out everything was getting paid car notes, rent, and bills. That's why the bitches surrounded him as if he was the last man on earth.

"Hey Smoke," a soft voice came from behind him. "Can I get a dance?"

"Yeah, come on." The stripper instantly got in front of him and started dancing. She was touching his dick and licking his neck as Dej Loaf played on the radio.

That's my shawty. I like what you be doing with yo body,
can't nobody get this pussy wet yo
and can't nobody fuck me like you can,
yo, like you can.

She continued to shake her ass on his dick and she felt Smoke's dick getting harder and harder with every motion of her ass cheeks. The girl had a mask on her face trying to conceal her identity. Smoke didn't know who this girl was and didn't care, but Keisha was watching this mysterious girl hard. She knew exactly who this girl was, Choc!

"Nicole, you see this bitch over there doing all this dancing on Smoke and he ain't gave this hoe a dime? I knew she was a snake ass bitch, but I'm going play it cool," Keisha said.

"Hell no, bitch. Let me cut this hoe." Nicole was about that action.

"No bitch, sit yo high ass down. I got this. Plus, that ain't my man. I'm not tripping off that lil shit. I just know how to handle the bitch," Keisha said, looking Nicole straight in the eyes.

Nicole just sat back thinking to herself, I got something for this bitch. Keisha is not about to be around to save this bitch all the time.

"Bitch, look at all these balling ass niggas in the club, though. I'm about to make some money tonight," Keisha said while walking to the stage. Keisha had on a white thong, a white studded bra and some ten-inch heels. Keisha's makeup was nicely done by a makeup artist in the Chicago area called Beat Faces. The diamonds around her neck were glistening. Keisha walked on the stage, grabbed the mic, and said, "Who's ready to see a real bitch?"

All the niggas and bitches ran to the stage, everybody loved Keisha.

"Hey, Choc. I see you," Keisha continued taunting Choc and tossed the mic down. Choc stood there looking puzzled. Keisha's favorite song was playing, Young Thug check.

Smoke sat back and watched Keisha work the pole like no other he sent his mans to the stage with four racks and said when she's done give her this and tell her she's done for the night and to meet me at her crib. Nigga's was throwing money left and right but Keisha didn't care she wanted Smoke to come give her some attention. Feeling like shit Keisha finish dancing picked up her money as she was walking off the stage Smoke's homeboy, Chi, grabbed her arm. Keisha tried to snatch away from him.

"Hold on lil mama. Smoke told me to give this to you and to tell you that you're done for the night. You need to meet him at yo house."

Keisha was looking like nigga please, but she grabbed the money, went to the back and got dressed. She grabbed Nicole.

"Bitch, we're out."

Chapter two

This nigga out here tricking on these bitches like he doesn't have a
bitch at home. That's why I say I don't trust his ass now. Every time I
put my all into his motherfucking ass, he dogs me out. I'm a bad ass
bitch. I don't got time for this, but since he wants to play, let's play.
Lady Luck took her last sip out of her glass and walked out swiftly
without anyone noticing her so she thought.
Lady Luck took the long way home, lowered her windows down turned
on her music. Tank was playing on the radio. "I just want somebody
body to treat me like somebody body. All you got to do is love me for
me, baby."
Lady Luck let the music take control of her body. She thought to
herself, "Damn Smoke, why must we go through this?" She finally
pulled up to her five-bedroom, five-bathroom house. The house was
everything a woman could ask for. Smoke purchased it for her because
he wanted her somewhere safe and out the hood.
Lady Luck got out the car and walked into her house to end up laid out
on her white leather couch. "Damn, it's been a minute since I got some
dick," she said aloud. She picked up her phone, dialed the number, and
waited for a reply on the other end.
"Hey, Chi. Can you come over real quick? I need you to do something
for me."
Chi looked at Smoke and said, "Bro, I got to go. Moms need me."
"Alright, man. Hit me up." They shook each other's hands and Chi left.

Lady Luck was just dosing off until she heard a loud knock on the door. She ran to the door to let in Chi. "Fuck me, daddy," she sultrily whispered, ushering him into her home.

Chi picked her up, put her up on the breakfast bar, ripped her black Victoria secrets panties off, and placed his face in her wet juicy pussy. "Chi, you're better than him. Eat this pussy, baby," she encouraged. Chi stroked his tongue in and out of her pussy getting her nice and wet for his dick. He stood up, placed his long, thick dick in his hand, and played with her pussy before sticking it in her hot honeycomb.

"Oh Chi, fuck me," Lady Luck moaned. "Fuck me now!"

Chi stuck his dick in her pussy and with every thrust, Lady Luck screamed out in pleasure. "Oh, Chi baby! Fuck me, daddy!" Chi was fucking her so good, her toes were curling and her moaning got louder. "Chi, your body is so motherfucking sexy. Stroke this pussy daddy. I want more cum in this pussy. Oooh, baby. I'm about to cum. Please don't pull out. Cum in this pussy daddy and cum in it right now!" And chi did just that."

***

Choc was sitting in her cramped apartment, gazing out the window while smoking a cigarette. Her house was a mess, just like her life. Dirty dishes for a week piled on top of her sink, pots, and pans with old food in it was scattered across the stove, roaches were running across the floor and her house smelled like cat piss. Choc had some dirty block nigga laid out on the mattress that was in the middle of the floor. "Get the fuck up nigga and go get some loud. We got some shit to discuss." Choc sat there waiting for her friend, Gunz, to come back when she heard her door open.

"Gunz, that's you?" she shouted. There was no answer. Choc walked to the door, but no one was there. "Now, I know that I heard somebody at the door." Choc looked in the hallway and wasn't anybody there. She walked back off thinking to herself, *this nigga can't do shit right but hit stains.* Choc walked over to her chair by the window to sit back down when she heard a big bang at the door.

"Damn, what the fuck? Who is it?" she yelled.

"Gunz bitch, open the door."

"Damn nigga, it took you long enough. Now, roll up!" she commanded.

"Now nigga, let's talk. I need to get that bitch, Keisha. I want her dead.

That bitch doesn't think that shit can happen to her. I know that bitch's every move," she began to plot.

Gunz took a long puff off the loud blunt. "So, what do I get out the deal?" he asked, passing the blunt back to Choc.

"Nigga, you get this pussy. So, are you going to kill this bitch or what?" she asked.

"Come suck this dick while I think about it," he smartly replied.

Choc instantly stood up, set Gunz down on the chair, and sucked his dick. She was a beast with the head. She sucked dick better than Super Head. "Damn girl, this shit feels so good," Gunz mumbled.

Choc was high out of her mind. She didn't even notice that Gunz laced her weed with crack. Choc was so into sucking Gunz dick that she didn't notice Keisha walking from the back of her apartment to leave out the door. Keisha and Gunz made eye contact. Keisha put her finger over her lips and said, "Shh." Gunz winked his eye as Keisha left out the door.

***

"Oh my, doesn't it feel good to get some good dick for a change? I've tried to stop fucking with Chi a long time ago, but Smoke won't do right so I'll fuck his friend right," Lady Luck mumbled. She giggled at herself just thinking about how bad of a bitch she still was.

"Chi daddy, are you done? I have a few things to do today before it gets too late."

"Yea ma, come give me a kiss."

"Ok daddy," Lady Luck screamed out she ran into his arms and gave him a sloppy wet kiss.

"See you later baby. Aye, by the way, I had fun last night. Here's a couple of dollars make sure you get something nice courtesy of Smoke," she spoke, handing Chi a couple stacks. Lady Luck and Chi have been stealing from Smoke for years. Chi took the rolled-up money, got in his all-white Audi, and drove off.

Lady Luck went upstairs to take a hot bath and to think about what her next move was going to be. Lady Luck grabbed her makeup pouch. She kept her stash of heroin that she occasionally snorts in there as to not be caught up by anyone, especially Smoke. Lady Luck snorted a line soaked in the tub and that's when her mind started racing.

"Man, I got to get these bitches. Who the fuck do they think they are fucking up what I build? I have to figure out who these two bitches are." Lady Luck picked up her phone and called her private Investigator. "Yes. Hello, Brian. I have two people that I need you to get information on. I got three-grand for you," she offered up to the PI. "Yes ma'am, anything for you. Meet me at my office and wear those panties that I like," Brian spoke into the phone and then Lady Luck ended the call. She didn't know where to start, but knowing Smoke, he will slip up again and be caught with both of those bitches. She just hoped that he isn't caught with his dick out.

Lady Luck thought to herself while snorting another line, *let me get out this tub and go meet Brian. I need him to do this job like now and instead of the three grand, I'll give him some pussy instead.* Before she left, she called Smoke to see if he would answer. *This nigga still hasn't called a bitch back.* Lady Luck grabbed her phone she dialed Smoke number, but no answer.

"This nigga still not answering with his bitch ass," she spoke aloud.

***

Keisha couldn't believe what she just heard. She really wanted to go crazy knowing what Choc was planning to do to her. "This bitch wants me dead huh? Ok, let's play!"

Keisha's phone rang. "Hello!" she yelled into the phone.

"Damn, ma. Is everything cool?" It was Smoke.

"Yea, I'm good. Why, what's up?" she asked.

"Can a nigga slide through and come fuck with you for a minute?" he asked.

"I really don't Know if I-"

Smoke cuts her off, "I'm on my way," and then he hangs up on her.

"This nigga must think it's a fucking joke. I don't know what type of bitch this nigga thinks I am or what type of drug he's smoking, but I got a bigger fish to fry," she said aloud, looking at the screen and seeing that the call ended.

Keisha rolled up a blunt, poured her a glass of Redberry Cîroc and sat down on her sectional couch and turned on her TV to watch the news. She heard a knock on the door. "Who is it?" she asked.

"Open the door!" Smoke yelled out.

Yea, this nigga is tripping today. Keisha thought while getting up to open the door.

"What's up ma? You good? You look a little stressed."

"No, I'm straight. What's up though?"

"Shit, I wanted to come fuck with you but you seem like you're mad, so I'll leave."

Keisha said, "No, you can stay."

Smoke was standing there looking and smelling like a bag of money. He had just left the shop getting his dreads touched up. Smoke had on an all-white t-shirt with some true religion jeans and some all-white Ones. Keisha just wanted to sex Smoke all night, but she thought against it and decided to discuss Choc.

"Sit down, I need to talk to you about something. So, you remember the night of the party and the girl that was dancing on you? Well, that's my friend Choc. Well, my used to be my friend, should I say. The bitch is cutthroat. But anyway, she's been acting really funny lately to the point where I don't know who she is sometimes. So after the night of the party, I had my friend Nicole follow her home to see what she was on or to see if you were going to show up there. Not that I was stalking you, but the bitch has done me and a couple of our mutual friends dirty before so I wanted to see if you fell for her shit.

So, my friend Nicole FaceTime me and told me that Choc was meeting up with this local nigga named Gunz. That's all I really needed to know. Gunz is a nigga that do hits around the hood for a small fee. So, I ended up going over there the next morning. I stood in the hallway for a while to see if Gunz was going to come out," she goes on to tell the story.

Smoke was looking shocked. He thought to himself, *this lil bitch is a savage.*

"So, Gunz ended up coming out and I stopped him in his steps. I gave him a bag of loud and some crack to lace her shit with and a few hundred to get me in the house, so I can listen to what she had planned. I got in there and this bitch was so deep in her thoughts that she didn't know I was in her back room listening to her plot to kill me. Right now, this shit got me livid. All I'm asking you, Smoke, is are you ready to rock with me because shit is about to get real?" she finished her story.

Smoke gave her a half grin and said, "Shawty, I got you."

Keisha and Nicole were riding down I-90 going to Rockford, Illinois to pick up Red. Red was a cool ass chick, she was the true definition of a rider. The three girls needed to devise a plan on how to get rid of Choc. These three always knew it was business when they linked. They have dealt with many bitches in the past and now it was time to put their heads together and figure out a plan for Choc's grimy ass.

They were quiet the whole ride, both of them had a lot on their minds. They finally pulled up to Red's house. Red stepped out looking good as always, matching from head to toe. Red was a real hood bitch and when you put a price on it, she is down for whatever. She will kill a bitch quick.

"What's up, bitch?" Keisha and Nicole screamed out.

"What's up y'all? What's the word? Let's go get some drinks and chat it up," Red greeted her friends. They went to the bar to order drinks and Keisha filled them both in on what was going on with Choc.

"You mean to tell me that you were in the bitch's house the whole time she was plotting to kill you?" Red asked. Nicole and Red looked at Keisha like she was crazy. Keisha nodded her head yea and they all started laughing. "Bitch, you've always been the lay low type."

"Bitch, I want to torture that hating ass bitch. So, who is in?" Keisha asked. They all shook each other's hands to put it all together that they were all in for the takedown. First thing first, kidnap Choc's ass. They rode back to Chicago and got to Keisha's house. Keisha called Gunz and told him to meet her at the spot tomorrow at noon.

Keisha was tired and stressed, she needed to find something to get into so she called Smoke.

"What's up ma?" Smoke answered sounding a little tired.

"I need you bad, daddy."

"Yep, I'm on my way," Smoke said.

"Ok, let's get a room. I have company here."

"You want me to pick you up?" Smoke asked.

"Yes, please," Keisha said.

"Ok, I'm on my way."

Keisha went to the bathroom, took a bath, applied lotion to her body, and sprayed on her Guilty Gucci perfume. She put on her black bra and panties set, her 10-inch pumps and her trench coat. She had to set the mood, and best believe she was coming for the title.

Smoke pulled up to Keisha's house and blew his horn. Keisha walked out the house and Smoke couldn't stop looking at her. "Damn, she fine," he uttered.

Keisha got in the car and kissed Smoke on the lips. "Hey daddy, let's go." They pulled up to the Palmer House Hotel in Downtown Chicago and got a room. As soon as they got in the room Keisha dropped her coat and pushed Smoke on the bed. She unzipped his pants, pulled out his meaty dick and began to suck it as if her life depended on it. Keisha was a beast in the bed. She deep throated his dick so good and made sure her mouth stayed wet. She didn't need her hands at all; she was a pro with head. Keisha took her tongue and licked from the tip of Smoke's dick all the way down to his balls. Smoke was moaning so loud and his toes were curling. Keisha got up and sat on Smoke's face. He was shocked, but he didn't hesitate to stick his tongue out licking her pearl and sucking her pussy lips until she creamed all over his mouth. This wasn't something that he usually did. He tossed Keisha on her back, put her legs on his shoulders and with every thrust Keisha moaned, "Ummm, daddy," biting her bottom lip.

"Fuck me, daddy. This is your pussy. Fuck me, daddy. Harder, harder...mmm...right there." Keisha dug her nails into Smoke's back. She felt his dick throbbing in her pussy, so she pushed him off her and sucked his dick until he came in her mouth making sure that she swallowed every ounce of him.

"Arghh, girl! You're the best. Will you marry me?" Smoke yelled out as he came all in her mouth, making sure she got every single drop..

chapter three

Lil Wayne's *Love Me* blasted on the radio as Choc was cleaning her apartment, waiting for Smoke to come over. Keisha thought she was doing something, but here she was about to fuck her nigga and she's going to make sure he pays her. Choc was so happy, she was wiping counters down, washing dishes making sure that she cleaned up the house spotless for Smoke. She had on her booty shorts and a wife beater.

Bang! Bang! Bang!

"Who is it?" Choc screamed out.

"Smoke," he answered.

Choc ran to the door, opening it to find Smoke's sexy ass standing there. She opens the door and invited him inside.

"What's up, Smoke?"

"Shit chilling," he replied.

"What's up with you?" Smoke said while looking in every room in the house.

"What's wrong, nigga? No one is here but me and you."

"Ok cool, sit down," Smoke said.

"Why do I have to sit down Smoke?" she asked.

"Because I said so," he said with some authority.

"So you want to make some money, huh? Open your mouth!" Smoke put his dick in Choc's mouth. He fucked her mouth until he got nice and hard, then he bent her over and stuck his dick in her ass.

She screamed out in pain, "Stop Smoke, please. It hurts!"

"No bitch. You want this money, right?" he spoke as he fucked her harder. After a few more pumps, he stuck his dick in her pussy and fucked her some more until he busted a fat one.

Choc laid there crying in pain and humiliation.

"Here go fifty dollars," he said, tossing the cash on her floor, then left. He walked out the door and was shocked when he saw someone standing there with a gun. Shots were fired, bullets hit Smoke all over his upper body and his body fell. Choc ran to her door, looked down the hall, and no one was in sight.

Choc was scared out her mind when Smoke grabbed her arm. She thought he was dead, but surprisingly he was still moving.

"Bitch, you better not let me die. I would hunt you for the rest of your life, bitch." Choc spat on him and left him for dead. Her neighbor was looking out her door Choc didn't even know she was being watched. Police sirens rang out as Smoke laid there blanking in and out of consciousness.

"Sir, if you can hear me stay with us. Don't die. His heart rate is dropping; we have to get him to the hospital." They rushed Smoke to the Cook County Hospital.

They performed surgery on him and removed the bullets. He was very lucky to survive from those gunshot wounds. Once Smoke woke up, the police were asking him all type of questions that he had the answers to but he wasn't telling them shit. Smoke knew exactly who shot him. As the police were leaving, Smoke called them back and said, "Can you let the doctor know that I don't want anybody to know I'm here? If anybody calls, I want to remain anonymous."

"Ok, sir. I'll let the doctor know." The police weren't believing anything Smoke was saying, but it wasn't anything they can do if he wasn't willing to assist them with the information to catch the shooters. Keisha's sister-in-law, Katrina, called her and told her that somebody had got shot in front of Choc's apartment. She sat up in her bed thinking, *What the fuck is going on?* She called Gunz to check on him. As Gunz picked up his phone, Keisha yelled into the phone, "Nigga, who the fuck got shot in front of Choc's crib? They said that it was a nigga."

Nicole ran into Keisha's room screaming, "Bitch, Smoke just got shot in front of Choc's crib." Keisha looked very shocked. She hung up the phone with Gunz and asked Nicole what was Smoke doing at Choc's crib anyway.

Keisha got up, put on her Love pink shirt and jogging pants with her pink Timberlands. She grabbed her thirty-eight off her dresser and headed for the door. Keisha, Nicole, and Red got in a stolen car and went straight to Choc's house. They sat outside and watched the police wrap up their investigation.

"I'm about to kill this bitch," Keisha said while punching the steering wheel.

"Calm down, bitch," Red said from the back seat.

Nicole sat in the passenger seat quietly. She spotted Choc getting in the car with another female. Nicole looked at Keisha asking, "Bitch, did Choc just get in that black car with the tinted windows?"

Keisha pulled off, started following them down the street. Choc and the girl pulled up in front of a nice house in Richton Park, Illinois. Keisha parked a couple cars down so they couldn't be noticed. They watched Choc get out the car with some pretty lady that they had never seen before.

"Damn, who is that bitch?" Red asked.

"Man, I don't know who she is but that bitch is bad," Nicole said.

"How did Choc get to know somebody in this good ass neighborhood? Something is not right." Keisha watched closely as if she was studying for a test. She waited until Choc and the lady finally gets in the house. She pulled up slowly in front of the house to get a closer look. Keisha's eyes got big when she saw all of Smoke's cars parked in front of the driveway.

"Girl, what?" Red asked her. Keisha said nothing and drove off. Choc and Lady Luck sat at the table conversing.

"So, did Smoke die?" Lady Luck asked her.

Choc sat there with a straight face and said, "Yea, he died. Now, can you pay me?"

"Yea, hold on. Let's have a drink first," Lady Luck offered.

Choc sat down and waited for Lady Luck to fix her a drink. She handed Choc her drink and she tossed it back quickly, she wanted to get this over with as soon as possible and be on her way. She instantly started feeling light-headed. She started to stand, but her legs were weak. Now, her head started to spin.

Lady Luck walked in, handed Choc an envelope that contained five-grand and a note that said, "Got you, bitch." Lady Luck smacked Choc with a pistol, instantly knocking her out. She grabbed Choc, tied her up, taped her mouth shut and dragged her down to the basement.

Keisha walked into her bedroom, poured her some Cîroc, and lit her blunt. She couldn't believe what was happening. What the fuck was Choc doing with Smoke's bitch? This shit is crazy. Keisha wasn't the type to tell her friends everything, so she kept a lot of shit to herself until the time was right. What is even crazier is trying to figure out what the fuck Smoke was doing at Choc's crib in the first place. She picked up her phone to call Gunz and she saw a text from Smoke's phone number.

Smoke: *Baby girl, I'm ok.*

Smoke was sitting on his hospital bed talking to his lawyer about faking his death. He told his lawyer that he knows who tried to kill him and that he wanted to stay in hiding. Smoke had other intentions for the person who wanted him dead. He had been blowing Keisha's phone up trying to get in touch with her, to no avail. She wasn't answering for him at all. Keisha was still mad at Smoke for being at Choc's house and he knew it. "I guess it's time for me to start planning on how to get back at the motherfuckers who tried to kill me, but first I need to get that bitch Choc for setting me up," Smoke plotted aloud.

Keisha was up and out as soon as the sun had risen. She went to get her hair done for a private party that she was booked for later on that night. She was kind of skeptical about going because something didn't feel right a, and not only that all she wanted to do was kill everybody, even Smoke. Keisha was at the neighborhood shop called Me Me's. There you will are able to get all the gossip down to who's fucking whom, whose baby daddies not claiming their babies and down to the color of a bitch's panties.

Choc's sister, Peaches, walked into the shop handing out a missing person flier with Choc's face on it. Peaches looked at Keisha and rolled her eyes. Keisha didn't give a fuck about her sister. She looked at her as another mad bitch. What had her puzzled was that Choc was missing. All she wanted to do was kill Choc, so either that bitch is hiding or Smoke's girl is holding her hostage. *Maybe I'll call Smoke or go see him to fill him in and see what he says, Keisha thought.*

Lady Luck was using Choc for her own personal sex object. She would get high and go to the basement and use sex toys to fuck Choc and on some days, she would make Choc eat her pussy. This particular day Lady Luck went downstairs and Choc was laying down crying. Lady Luck walked up to her and kicked her in the stomach. "Bitch shut the fuck up. Were you crying when you were fucking my nigga? Were you crying then?" she asked.

Choc didn't respond. She was always a fighter, but this type of torture she wasn't prepared for at all. She could only think about Keisha and how good Keisha had been to her. Karma has finally caught up with her.

"Can you just kill me? I don't deserve to live," Choc whispered.

"Bitch, kill you? That will be too easy. Chi and I have so much more planned for you," Lady Luck said.

Choc looked up and said, "You bitches."

Keisha woke up the next afternoon with the mindset to kill or be killed. She knew she was going to kill whoever stood in her way. She wanted the bitch Choc badly, but she wanted to do this with no help. She decided to text Smoke and put some pieces to the puzzle together.

Keisha: *So how did you manage to get shot in front of Choc's crib?*

Smoke: *I was there to kill her*

Can she trust him anymore? Everything that came out of his mouth seemed to be a lie.

Keisha: *Just say you were there to fuck the bitch and got caught with yo dick out.*

Keisha didn't text back, she decided to go up to the hospital just to find out he wasn't there and they had no record of him even being in the hospital.

Keisha: *Smoke, where are you? I'm at the hospital and they're telling me you have never been to this hospital. What's going on?*

Smoke still didn't text back. Keisha stood there and for the first time in a long time, she felt hurt. Tears started flowing down her face. She was wondering why he would do this to her.

"Fuck it," Keisha said. She got up and left out and her phone started ringing. It was Gunz.

"What's up Keisha? I got some info for you," Gunz spoke into the phone.

"Ok, I'll be there in a minute." Keisha left the hospital without looking back. she finally got to the project complex and Gunz was sitting on the bench smoking a blunt. He asked Keisha if she wanted a hit.

"No, I'm cool. What's up doe?" she asked.

"Aye, word on the street is that Chi shot Smoke and Smoke's bitch is fucking Chi," he informed her.

"Who the fuck is Chi?" Keisha asked.

"That's Smoke right-hand man and to top it off, they're looking for you. His bitch, Lady Luck, wants you dead. You have to be careful fucking with her, she is very good at what she does. I mean our next move has to be very silent," he went on to explain.

Keisha reached into her pockets to pay him, but he stopped her. Gunz said, "I'm straight, lil momma. This shit is personal now."

Gunz was sitting in his small apartment that was well put together, contemplating on how he was going to get back at Lady Luck for killing their baby. Gunz wasn't always just a regular hitman. He used to be paid until he got into smoking dope. He had met Lady Luck before she became Smoke's, First Lady. He knew her when she didn't have shit but a hope and a dream. Gunz and Lady Luck were the perfect couple, so he thought. He later learned that she wasn't anything but a bitch with a pussy that killed their first child.

"I'm going to kill that bitch when I see her. I'm going to cut her fucking head off and feed it to my dog," Gunz said with anger. He thought Lady Luck was dead this whole time. Keisha sent a text to Gunz.

Keisha: *What's up nigga, you ready?*

Keisha stood in her living room talking to Nicole and Red. "Man, we need to go out," Red said.

"Yeah bitch, when I get back let's hit up Red Diamond Strip Club," Keisha said.

"Hell yea, I'm down. It's been a long time since I was able to shake this ass," Nicole yelled from the other side of the room.

"Where are you about to go, Keisha?" Red questioned.

"Girl, about to meet this nigga really quick and wrap my lips around his dick," Keisha lied.

"Yea ok, call me when you on your way back." She knew Keisha wasn't keeping it real, so she decided to follow her.

chapter four

Keisha's sister, Katrina, and Red sat at Keisha's house smoking loud, talking, and playing spades. "Man, this club better be popping tonight," Red said. Red's phone started to ring it was Keisha.

"Hello," Red said.

"Bitch, y'all better be ready tonight. I'm so ready to turn up-"

Beep, beep, beep.

"Hold on, somebody is behind me blowing their horn," Keisha yelled out the window. "What the fuck? Go around if you in a rush, stupid bitch." The car slammed on the gas hit the back of Keisha's car.

"Whoever this is, is trying to kill me," she told Red who was still on the phone. The car hit the gas again, this time hitting the back of Keisha's car and sending her car into a ditch. The car took off after that.

"Keisha! Keisha!" Red yelled out. "Bitch, stop playing. What's going on?" Keisha's phone went dead. Red looked at Katrina and said, "Something just happened to Keisha." They ran out the house as Nicole was coming in the door.

"What's going on? Y'all bitches look like death," Nicole asked.

"Something just happened to Keisha!" Red yelled.

"What do you mean something just happened to Keisha?" she asked in a panic.

"Bitch, somebody was just ramming the back of her car. All I heard was a loud noise like she crashed and then her phone went dead."

"Let's go ride around to see if we can see what's up," Nicole said.

Katrina's phone rang, it was Keisha's grandma.

"Baby, your sister-in-law is in the hospital in critical condition. The doctors say she might not make it."

Smoke was sitting back watching the news, he couldn't believe what he just saw.

"Girl left in critical condition after being run off the road near the Dan Ryan Expressway."

He'd seen Keisha's car being pulled out the ditch and all kinds of emotions filled his body. "Fuck man, I should have never left her out there." Smoke punched the wall leaving a big hole. He jumped right in his car and drove to the home he shared with Lady Luck.

"Ooh daddy, fuck me." Lady Luck was on top of Chi, riding his dick from the back. "Oh, I want all this dick. Do you like how this pussy feel on that dick, daddy?"

Chi grabbed Lady Luck's ass cheeks and said, "Whose pussy is this?" and before Lady Luck can answer, the door flung open. Smoke pulled out his gun and pointed it at Chi and told him to get up.

"That's how you do me? You're supposed to be my motherfuckin right-hand, and you bitch, you're fucking this nigga in the house that I paid for and put your nothing ass in. Tie him up now," Smoke demanded.

Lady Luck grabbed the rope and did as she was told. She tied Chi up as tight as she could and then taped his mouth shut. Smoke looked at him and said, "Look how quick this bitch turned on you. She ain't anything but a dope head ass bitch."

Lady Luck looked at him surprised. She didn't know that he knew about her drug addiction.

"Yeah bitch, you thought I didn't know." He slapped the shit out of her in the mouth, her whole head spun around and she fell to the floor. "Get up, bitch, and help me take this nigga to the truck."

Lady Luck got up and attempted to pull Chi. "I can't he is too heavy," she whined.

"Bitch, grab him!" Smoke smacked Lady Luck across the head with his pistol. She screamed out in pain. "Get him to the truck, bitch!" They were finally able to get Chi to the truck. Smoke drove to an open field and once there, he got out the car, walked over to the back seat, opened the door and as soon as he was about to shoot Chi, Lady Luck pulled out a blade and cut Smoke across the ear.

"Bitch, did you just cut me?" he grabbed Lady Luck by the neck and choked her until she turned blue. He grabbed his gun as soon as he was about to pull the trigger, he notices a car creeping up on them. Smoke snatched Chi out his seat, got back in his car, turned the lights off, and drove off slowly but he was still watching Lady Luck and Chi through his window. Whomever that was that got out the car had shot Chi and Lady Luck and cut their body parts up. Smoke couldn't believe what he just witnessed. He knew exactly who the bitch was, but was unsure of how she knew that he brought them there.

Keisha laid in her hospital bed with tubes in her nose, and her eyes were closed shut. Red and Katrina were at her bedside and no one knew where Nicole was currently.

Red said, "Damn, Nicole has been disappearing a lot lately.

Katrina said, "Yea she has. She's starting to make me believe she has something to do with my sister laying up in the hospital."

The doctor came in the room to inform Keisha's family that they might have to pull the plug. Katrina went crazy and started fighting the doctor and nurses so bad that she had to be removed from the floor. You could still hear her crying and screaming, "How am I supposed to tell her brother this?"

Red was speechless. She pulled the doctor to the side to see if there was anything that they could do to assist with her injuries and healing.

"Man, please give her a couple of days. I know she can pull through," Red pleaded with him. The Doctor walked out the room and said, "It's not my decision."

Red walked to Keisha and held her hand. She spoke to her, willing her strength and perseverance, "Keisha, you have to pull through man. It's not your time, G. Pull through, ma." Just then Red heard, "Breaking news," and looked up at the TV.

"Hi, my name is Maria from the Channel Seven News. We are reporting that two bodies were found dead in the middle of a field on the city's West Side. The bodies that were discovered were also dismembered and the identities of these two victims are being withheld due to the pending family notification."

Keisha grabbed Red's hand hard, but she never opened her eyes. Red left the hospital with a lot on her mind. She decided to call Nicole to see where she was so that she could inform her of Keisha's status. Her phone rang three times and then went to voice mail. Red tried to call again, this time it went straight to voicemail. "What the fuck man? Where are you, Nicole?" Red said to herself, walking into the bar. She needed to take a shot and take the edge off. She sat next to two loud ghetto girls. They were talking about Smoke.

"Girl, I heard that nigga Smoke wasn't dead. Shit, I even heard he had his bitch, Lady Luck, and his homie, Chi, killed. He was supposed to walk in on them fucking, but I think the real reason he had them killed was that they were trying to kill that Keisha bitch."

Red couldn't believe what she was hearing. She got up and left. All she wanted to do was talk to Keisha. "I'm about to kill every fucking body that I feel like had something to do with my G laying up in the hospital dying. I need to find that bitch, Nicole."

Nicole had to lay low now considering what she has done. She knows she left without saying anything and that's because she didn't want anybody to get in her way for what she had planned. Killing Lady Luck and Chi were the best things she could have done. She didn't know what she was going to do without Keisha if she died and the only thing she could do right now is hold Choc hostage until Keisha gets better. That way they can finish their original plans were and find out who tried to run her off the road. *I hope that Smoke didn't see me that night...*

Keisha laid in her hospital bed in deep thought; no one knew she was really awake. She needed to play dead to stay out the way of everybody that crossed her. Keisha knew that when she got out of the hospital she was killing everybody, including Nicole. No one knew where Nicole was and it was time for her to wake the fuck up now. When Keisha started coughing her grandma jumped up in shock, ran in the lobby, and yelled for the doctor. The doctor went into Keisha's room and to his surprise her eyes were open. She was still coughing.

"Get her some water!" Doctor Thompkins yelled out. The nurse brought Keisha some water and she gulped it down with one swallow. They cleared out her room and began to ask a series of questions. The Fox News crew came in to interview her. One reporter asked Keisha if she knew who ran her off the road.

She replied with her eyes looking directly into the camera, "Yes, I do..."

Nicole was at her house in Indiana that nobody knew about. She turned her phone off because everybody was blowing her up, especially Red.

Nicole was going to call her, but not right now. She had Choc tied up to a bed in the other room. Nicole decides to roll up a blunt and listen to Dreezy's mixtape. The first song that came on was "Chiraq." Nicole was in her zone listening to this song getting high out her mind. She pulled out her phone to turn it back on and a slew of missed calls, tons of text messages and voicemails were awaiting her. Nicole opened up the first text message and it was from Red.

Red: Bitch, where are you at?

Red: Nicole, I'm getting worried.

Red: Bitch, I'm going to kill you.

Nicole got very irritated and called Red, but this time Red didn't pick up the phone. "What the fuck does she want to kill me for? I don't see her out here putting in know work. I'm trying to make sure these bitches are off the street," she spoke aloud. She called Red again, no answer. She left a voicemail this time. "Bitch, what's up? You're tripping!" Nicole yelled into the phone.

Nicole turned on the news to see Keisha's face all over it. She got excited and nervous at the same time because if Red thought she'd tried to kill her, so would Keisha. She doesn't need that type of war, so she picked up her phone to dial Keisha's number and to her surprise, Keisha picked up the phone.

"Bitch, you're dead. You tried to kill me," Keisha said, and the phone went dead.

"I can't believe this shit," Nicole said. Reaching for her nine-millimeter, she went into the other room with Choc and put the gun to her head. "This is all your fault. Bitch, if you would've kept your legs closed and played by the rules, we wouldn't be going through this shit." She hit Choc upside her head with the gun.

Choc started to chuckle. "Let me guess. Your little friend, Keisha, wants you dead." Choc started laughing.

"Shut up bitch before I blow your brains out." Nicole shoved the gun in Choc's mouth. As soon as she was about to pull the trigger, Smoke kicked in Nicole's door.

He followed Nicole back to her place after she killed Lady Luck and Chi. Nicole turned around as quick as she could and locked eyes with the devil himself. Nicole walked up on Smoke with the gun in her hand and put the gun to his head. Smoke looked at her and said, "Lil Mama, put that gun down if you're not about to use it. I'm just here to help you, so you can help me get closer to Keisha."

"Boy, you're crazy. She's not fucking with me, so what makes you think I can even get close to her? She thinks I tried to kill her."

Smoke heard a bump he walked behind Nicole and noticed Choc hiding on the side of the bed. "Just the bitch I've been looking for. How the fuck did you get this bitch? I've been looking all over for her. Untie her."

"Hell no, I'm not about to untie her. Nigga, are you crazy?" Nicole exclaimed.

"Untie this bitch," he spoke with more authority.

"Hell no. Nigga, you untie her." Nicole kept her gun close.

Smoke untied Choc. She starts to beg for her life. "Please don't kill me, Smoke. I'm sorry," Choc screamed. Luckily, they were in the middle of nowhere because the way Choc was screaming, someone would have heard her.

"Bitch, I told you that I was going to kill you. Didn't I? But before I do that I want you to tell me how the fuck did you manage to set me up. I thought you just wanted some of this dick, but apparently, you wanted my life." Nicole just shook her head.

"Nicole, call Keisha right now. If she doesn't answer, send a pic of me and this nasty bitch Choc," Smoke yelled out.

Nicole did what she was told, but deep down inside she wanted to kill Smoke and Choc. She sent a text to Keisha.

Nicole: Bitch, I tried to tell you what was going on, but you didn't want to listen. Now, Smoke is here and I think he's going to kill Choc and me.

***

Red was sitting at Keisha's kitchen table eating breakfast. She called Keisha into the kitchen so that she can eat breakfast and talk because they both had a lot of catching up to do. Keisha broke the silence. "So, Nicole called me last night." Red almost choked on her juice.

"Bitch, you're lying."

"Nope. She called me, but I didn't give her a chance to talk. I just basically told her that I was going to kill her," Keisha replied.

"Damn G, you think she really wanted you dead? I'm starting to think differently. Why would she even call you? Plus, when I left the hospital, I went to the bar and two bitches were saying Smoke killed

Lady Luck and Chi because he thinks they tried to kill you. So now, I'm thinking differently about Nicole having anything to do with trying to kill you," Red said while eating a piece of bacon.

"To be honest Red, I don't know if she did or if she didn't. I'm just trying to figure out why she wasn't there for me in my time of need," Keisha said, attempting to put the pieces of the puzzle together. Red picked up her phone and called Nicole still no answer.

"Why is she not answering? She's making herself look real suspect. Something isn't right about this shit. What the fuck is going on? No need to sit around, it's time to make some moves," Red stated.

Red interrupted her rant, "Oh yea, I forgot to tell you. The word on the street is that Smoke is out here going crazy trying to find you.

Keisha started laughing. "Bitch, I don't care. Fuck that nigga. He'd better hope that I don't fucking kill him."

She walked into her room to get her phone and to her surprise, it was a text from Nicole. All she could do was scream, "Red, bitch, come here now. Shit just got real!"

Chapter five

Gunz was on a mission to find Keisha before she found him. "Damn, I
should have killed her ass. Now, she knows it was me that ran her off
the road. How can I be so fucking sloppy?" Gunz took a pull of his
Newport. "I knew she was going to try to handle Lady Luck before I
can get a chance to murk the bitch, so I had to knock out the
middleman. Shit, but by me doing that I failed at killing her. Someone
took the pleasure that I would have had of killing Lady Luck, but
somebody got to the bitch before I did," Gunz spoke aloud.
"Now, I'm out here dry and ready to kill Keisha before she kills me."
He took another pull from his Newport. He walked into his room to get
his gun that he never goes anywhere without. He got a knock on the
door.
"Who is it?"
"Chicago Police Department, open up," an officer yelled.
Gunz started tweaking. What the fuck? What the fuck?
"Open the door before we kick it in," one of the officers yelled.
Gunz tossed his gun out the window. He went to open the door and to
his surprise, it was two big niggas, Richard and King, Keisha's uncles.
Gunz didn't know what to do. It was no way that he could fight both of
these niggas, not even one on one. King punched Gunz in the face
knocking him out. They wrapped him up, put him in the trunk, and took
him to the West Side of Chicago to a basement they used to torture.
Once they got there, they called Keisha to let her know that they
handled that business she'd asked them to do for her and that they'll

take care of him until she got there. Gunz heard them on the phone and all that he could do was shake his head. He knew that he would not come up out of this alive.

"What was your reason to want my niece dead, nigga?" Richard asked. Without giving Gunz a chance to answer, he hammered a nail through his hand.

"Grrrrr," Gunz moaned.

"Oh nigga, you're in pain now huh?" King asked drilling nails into each one of Gunz's fingers.

"I'm sorry, please stop. I'll do anything," Gunz screamed like a bitch.

"Nigga, you weren't screaming when you were trying to kill my fam."

"I promise that it wasn't only me."

Richard took out his gun and pistol-whipped Gunz until he was knocked out cold. Keisha called her Uncle King and said, "Man, y'all need to meet me. Nicole just sent me a text and she has Choc held hostage. Smoke somehow found her and ran in her crib on some help me help you type shit. I don't trust this shit at all."

"So, what do you want me to do about this nigga?" King asked.

"Blow his brains out and bury him. Make sure y'all toss them phones," Keisha said. King walked up on Gunz and shot him in his face and they buried him with all the other dead bodies they had accumulated in the past.

"Alright let's go meet Keisha and see what's up with this situation," King said, they got in their car and went to Keisha spot but didn't know they were being followed.

Keisha sat there waiting for her uncles to arrive. They finally arrived and she was elated.

"Man, what's up Uncs? Y'all took care of that business for me, right?" she asked.

"Yea, we did that for you," King responded

Keisha grabbed her phone and dialed Nicole's number. Nicole picked up the phone sounding frantic.

"Hello? Bitch, get here now. This nigga, Smoke, is over here tripping. He said if you don't come, he's going to kill me and Choc."

Keisha started laughing. "Girl, put that nigga on the phone." Nicole walked into the other room to hand Smoke the phone.

"Smoke, it's Keisha," she announced.

Smoke jumped up so fast and snatched the phone from Nicole. "Hello baby, this you?"

"Yea, I'm on my way nigga. Tell Nicole to text me the address." She hung up with Smoke. "I'm finna kill all of these motherfuckers."

Keisha sat around waiting for Nicole to text her the address. Finally, thirty minutes later Nicole sent a text to Keisha's phone.

"Okay y'all, let's go. It's game time." They all got in their cars and left. King and Richard got in their car and followed Keisha and the person who was following Keisha's uncles were now following them. The ride seemed like it would never end. Keisha's head was spinning; so many emotions and thoughts ran through her mind. She wanted to love Smoke, but another part of her wanted him dead.

"Red?"

"What's up, Keisha?"

"I don't know if I want to kill Smoke. A part of me wants to be loved by him," she spoke her thoughts.

"Bitch, whatever you do I'm behind you a hundred percent. Whatever we do Choc has to die tonight," Red said.

"Hell yeah, bitch. Rock-a-bye, baby." Keisha started laughing. They finally pulled up to the address. It was pitch black and Keisha instantly grabbed her gun. Keisha and Red got out of the car first and walked up to the door. They twist the doorknob and the door creeks open.

Keisha walks in first with her gun drawn. She couldn't hear a sound.

Red whispers, "Bitch, why the fuck is it so quiet and dark up in this bitch?"

"Shh," Keisha said. Smoke was watching their every move.

"Keisha!" Smoked yelled out.

Keisha turned around and locked eyes with Smoke. *Damn, he looks good.*

"Put the gun down, Keisha," Smoke ordered.

"I'm not putting shit down, nigga. What the fuck I look like to you? A clown ass bitch?" Keisha cocked her pistol and as soon as she was about to pull the trigger, she felt a gun pressed to her temple.

A woman's voice said, "I wouldn't do that if I was you."

Keisha turned around to see Red being held at gunpoint by some ugly nigga and Choc's sister Peaches standing there with fire in her eyes.

"Bitch, where the fuck is my sister?"

31

Keisha looked at Peaches and started laughing. "What the fuck you asking me for bitch? I'm trying to find that hoe too." Peaches smacked Keisha with the gun. "Bitch, your entourage won't be here helping you tonight. They're having car troubles." Peaches slashed her uncles' tires, so they weren't able to be there to help Keisha. Smoke was standing there speechless. He didn't know what the fuck was going on. He finally spoke, "If you bitches want to live, put the fucking guns down, or no one will be leaving out of this bitch alive tonight."

Nicole crept up behind the dude that was holding a gun to Red's head and blew his brains out all over the place. As soon as he hit the floor, Keisha was laying blow after blow to Peaches face.

"You're a stupid ass bitch. You should've stayed out of this," Keisha spoke with anger as she punched Peaches in the mouth knocking her teeth out. If anybody knew about Keisha, they should've known that she was a fighter. Keisha has stood toe to toe with some of the best of them. Keisha was beating Peaches so bad Red had to get in between them and break them up.

"Don't fucking touch me," Keisha yelled. She picked Peaches up by her throat and choked her until Peaches blanked out. She let Peaches' body drop to the floor with a loud thud. Keisha yelled, "Where the fuck is Choc?" looking Smoke in his eyes with hatred.

Smoke wasn't moved at all; Keisha didn't scare Smoke.

"She's in the basement."

They all walked to the basement and Choc was gone.

"What the fuck?" Nicole yelled out as they ran back upstairs to look for her and to their surprise Peaches was gone. They heard a car speeding off. Keisha was livid.

"How the fuck did my plan to kill this bitch go down the drain?" She looked at Smoke, pulling her gun out. "It's all your fault. You went to fuck her."

chapter six

Silence filled the room. "Keisha, remember what we just talked about on our way here? Just give him time to explain," Red attempted to diffuse the situation.

"Man, fuck this nigga. He got what he wanted, I'm just another bitch to him," Keisha spat. Nicole sat there silently waiting to see if Smoke was going, to tell the truth about what happened between him and Choc. Smoke sat down and began to talk. Keisha walked towards him. She stood directly in front of him and looked him straight in the eyes and said, "Don't lie to me," with tears still flowing from her eyes. Smoke grabbed her hand and Keisha snatched her hand away from him. Smoke put his head down and started to speak, "I fucked her, but it wasn't like that."

"What do you mean it wasn't like that?"

"Keisha, I love you. Please give me another chance with you. I didn't mean to hurt you."

"Nigga, if you love me then why would you fuck Choc after I poured my heart out to you? I told you how I felt about her, but you still went to her house to fuck and ended up being shot. This is all your fault," Keisha said. She smacked Smoke in the face, grabbed her keys, and left. This time Nicole and Red followed behind her. Smoke wasn't about to stop fighting for Keisha's love. He was going to give her time to think.

***

Choc and Peaches were riding down I-95. The drive was quiet. Peaches pulled into a hotel on the city's low end. Peaches was in horrible pain; her mouth was leaking so much blood. She tried to clean herself up before going to check into the hotel, she didn't want the front desk clerk getting suspicious.

Choc was on the passenger side, she had lost a lot of weight being held captive. She turned to her sister and said, "Thank you." Peaches and Choc never really seen eye to eye, but when they were younger they promised to be there for one another considering all that they have been through. Choc was always overprotective when it came down to her little sister. They went through hell with their parents. every time Peaches would get in trouble by her dad, Choc would always step up to take whatever was coming. That's why Peaches felt like she had to be there for her sister.

Peaches finally cleaned herself up to get ready and go check into the hotel. They get to their room, Choc ran her some bath water, sat there and soaked for hours thinking about changing her life around. *I can't keep living my life like this. I was damn near dead. Being disloyal really showed me a lot.* Choc finally got out the tub. She called Peaches in there to help her out, she was really sore and weak.

Peaches ran into the bathroom, she looked at her reflection in the mirror and got very angry. Four of her top teeth were missing, her mouth was swollen, and both eyes were black. Peaches looked at Choc and said, "I'm going to kill Keisha!"

Choc didn't want to tell her sister just yet that she was leaving Chicago for good. Choc couldn't live her life like this anymore. *I'm ready for a new life,* Choc thought. *I can't see myself being a savage ass bitch all my life.*

Peaches looked at Choc and asked, "Why aren't you saying anything? You don't want to kill this bitch now? Look at us!"

That bitch Keisha has to die Choc I'm not about to play with this bitch. yo motherfucking ass needs to get better so we can kill her and them bitches she roll with, if you not down then I'll do it myself Choc just walked off and went to sleep...

***

Keisha was on the other side of town and it was just starting to get cold outside, so Keisha turned on her fireplace. She sat in front of the fire reading "King Divas" by De'nesha Diamond and drinking her Patron.

Nicole walked into the room where she was and said, "Can we talk?"
"Yea, I guess," Keisha said rolling her eyes. She sat up and stared at Nicole.
"What?" Nicole sat down next to her.
"I know that we've been kind of on edge these past couple of days. I just wanted to say that you can trust me. I never left you. I was just trying to be there for you throughout this whole ordeal. I know how you get when you want to do shit by yourself, so I followed you everywhere to make sure you were good. I killed Lady Luck and Chi." Keisha just looked at her and laid back down. Nicole walked off as Red was coming in the room.
"What's going on, bitch?" Red asked.
"Nothing, I'll be back later." Nicole left and went to her boyfriend's house for the rest of the night.
"What the fuck is wrong with Nicole?" Red asked.
"Nothing, she's just trying to do the right thing now. I wish she would've kept it a hunnit with me from the get-go," Keisha said.
"Well, you know how you can get when somebody gets in your way," Red said while hitting the blunt.
"I don't need the Martin Luther King speech." They both started laughing.
"So, what you got planned, bitch because I'll be leaving soon? You know I have to go back home to make sure everything is straight with my house," Red said.
"Yea bitch, I know. I think I'm about to lay low, stack some more money, and then find that bitch, Choc. I still want her dead-"
Red interrupted, "Why did you beat that bitch Peaches' ass like that? Bitch, you were knocking in that hoe's head."
"Bitch, shut the fuck up and pass the blunt, but on a serious note, I have to find Choc. I am going to blow her fucking brains out and piss on her grave." Keisha's phone rang and it was Smoke's ass. She sent him to voicemail. "I wish this nigga stop calling me. I'm about to set his ass up, he fucked with the right bitch."
Smoke was on the other side of town getting all his businesses back in order. He figured since everybody was dead, he'd show his face in the hood. Everybody kept asking him how he was doing and telling him that they were sorry for his loss, but what they didn't know was that he

didn't care. Smoke picked up his phone and called Keisha. She pressed the end button, so he left her a voicemail.

"Aye Shawty, enough is enough. Call me before I find you."

Some big booty girl walked up to Smoke.

"Aye, you know where the loud at?"

Smoke sized her up; he couldn't believe how beautiful this girl was.

"You look like you're too young to be smoking."

"Maybe, but why are you worried about it? The last time I checked, the nigga that fucked my mama and help produce me was at home. Now, do you know where it's at or not?"

"Nah shawty, I don't," Smoke responded.

"My name is not Shawty. It's Re-Re. The next time you see me, say that instead of shawty," she smartly responds and walks off. Smoke just looked at her and shook his head.

Red finally was getting ready to go back home. She stopped to get gas. As she gets out of her car, she never noticed that someone was following her.

"Aye, you remember me?" It was Choc's sister and a big nigga named Zo. He grabbed Red, put a bag over her head, and tossed her in the trunk.

chapter seven

Nicole went back to Keisha's house to see if Red was there. Red wasn't answering her phone and Nicole was worried. Nicole let herself in with the spare key she had. She walked over there to Keisha asking, "Have you heard from Red?"

"Yep, she went home. Why?" Keisha said with an attitude.

"She ain't been answering her phone, that's why. You need to chill out with your fucking attitude bitch because I ain't did shit to you but help," Nicole yelled. She got in Keisha's face. "Remember who's been here since day one before you start acting stupid. I'm still that same bitch though," Nicole said, as she walked towards the door. She turned around and tossed Keisha's key at her.

Keisha yelled at Nicole, "You're a stupid ass bitch."

Nicole walked out the door and said, "Fuck you."

"Man, this bitch is tripping. She's acting like I did something to her. Fuck Nicole, man," Keisha said while breaking her weed down. Her phone rang and it was Smoke.

"Hello?" Keisha answered.

"What's up ma?" he asked.

"Shit. Can you stop calling me?" she sassed, trying to get her point across that she didn't want to be bothered.

Keisha hung up the phone. *I'm tired of this fugazi ass nigga.* She finished rolling her weed, put on Rich Homie Quan's "Type of Way," stood by the window and smoked her blunt.

I need to get the fuck out of this house. Even though it was cold outside the sun was shining. Keisha put on her black Levi's, black tee and her black Hoodie with her black Timbs. She brushed her hair into a messy bun, put her Gold hoop earrings on and shined lips with her favorite lip gloss. She grabbed her Gucci bag and her chrome nine-millimeter from off the dresser.

Keisha walks out the door, "Shit, it's cold out here, and this nigga won't stop calling me. I should go shoot his ass in the fucking face." Keisha laughed. She pulled up in front of the Rothschild Liquor Mart on 63rd and Vernon Avenue.

"Aye, let me get a fifth of Red Berry Cîroc," she spoke to the clerk.

"Damn Keisha, where have you been?" She heard from behind her.

Keisha turned around to see her ex-boyfriend.

"Hey baby, I've been around." She leans in to give him a hug.

"Who the fuck is this bitch trying to hug you?" a woman's voice behind her said.

Keisha looked up and it was Peaches. Keisha pulled out her gun and aimed it the hoe's head.

"Well, well, well… Look who done came out of hiding. Bitch, you're by yourself now. I should beat your motherfucking ass."

Keisha looked at Peaches cocks her gun. "I would like to see you try it lil bitch. You'll be missing more than some teeth; you'll be missing your brain. Now, carry on you bum ass bitch because you ain't moving shit around here but your mouth. By the way, tell your sister that it ain't ova," Keisha said while leaving out the store. Peaches tried to run up on Keisha, but Zo grabbed her. "That's right Zo, grab that bitch while she still got the rest of her good teeth."

"What the fuck, Peaches? Why the fuck you didn't tell me that's who you were into it with? That bitch, Keisha, is crazy. Do you know her cousin? That bitch will have us dead! Tell me the bitch that we got held hostage don't have shit to do with Keisha? Tell me, Peaches!"

"Um, um, well," Peaches stuttered.

"Peaches, never mind. Let's go. I'll ask her my fucking self. Stupid ass bitch got me in some shit. I knew this shit was too good to be true. Man, this bitch better hope I don't kill her ass," Zo said.

They pulled up to an abandoned building, went to the trunk to get Red out and she was gone. They looked in the back seat and Red had kicked her way out. "Fuck!" Zo yelled. "This bitch got away."

Keisha was riding around the city listening to Lil Boosie's "Betrayed".
She decided to go to Smoke's hangout spot and get up with him.
"Damn, I wonder what this nigga is on."
As she walked into the spot on 87th and Lowe, she noticed Smoke
talking to some girl and they were all hugged up on each other.
This nigga is a fool with it. Let me order me a drink and go join the party.
"Aye, let me get a Cîroc on the rocks."
The bartender handed her drink and said, "Keep your money, this drink
is on me."
"Aww thank you, sweetie," Keisha said smiling as she walked over to
where Smoke was sitting. "Hey Smoke," she spoke. *Look at this nigga's face; priceless*, Keisha thought.
"Hi, my name is Keisha. I'm Smoke's cousin and you are?" Keisha
asked the no name girl that he was hugged up on while mugging the
shit out of Smoke.
"Awe, I'm Re Re. What's up Keisha?" Re Re spoke to Keisha.
"Oh, Re Re, can you go over there for a minute? I need to holler at
Smoke really quick." Re Re looked at Smoke for confirmation.
"It's cool. Go ova there," Smoke said.
"So Smoke, this is what you're doing? You are a dirty ass nigga. That's
why I can't fuck with you," Keisha said. She threw her drink in his
face. Smoke got up and grabbed Keisha around the waist.
"You want to act a fool, right? Let me the fuck go, Smoke, before I
beat yo ass."
Re Re walked back over to see what the hell was going with her new
male friend. "Is everything ok, Smoke?"
Keisha got loose and punched Re Re in the mouth. "It is now." Re Re
grabbed Keisha's hair throwing blow after blow. Keisha was eating
every punch. "Awe bitch, you're a fighter huh?" Keisha grabbed Re Re
by the throat, picked her up with one hand and with the other hand she
gave Re Re all face shots. "Bitch, I bet the next time you will mind
your fucking business. Right?"
That last punch Re Re screamed out in pain, "Arghhhh," and that's
when Smoke grabbed Keisha.
"Go the fuck home, now Keisha. You're tripping, ma, for real."

Keisha yanked away from Smoke, left out, got in her car, and drove off. Her phone rang and it was from an unknown number. She wasn't about to answer, but something told her to find out who was calling her. "Hello?" Keisha answered.

"Keisha, come get me now. This is Red. I'm on 55th and State. Hurry up, bitch."

"I'm on my way."

What the fuck is wrong with Red? Keisha did 70 on the dashboard trying to get to Red. Her head was pounding and it felt like her heart was gonna stop. Keisha finally got there and Red got in the car. She was silent at first and Keisha just stared at Red.

"It looks like we both just got into a brawl. What happened to you, bitch?" Red broke the silence.

Keisha told her what happen between her Smoke and the Re Re bitch. Red just shook her head, not being able to comprehend what the hell was going on today.

"What happen to you?" Keisha asked.

"Peaches called herself kidnapping me, bitch. She snatched me up at the gas station. Her and this big nigga, they trunked me, bitch, but I got out of that jam. I guess they thought I was an amateur," Red went on to explain.

"Get the fuck out of here, bitch. I'd just seen that hoe and my ex-boyfriend, Zo. That's probably who helped her," Keisha said.

"Call Nicole and tell her that time for war."

chapter eight

Nicole was laying down on her man's chest, watching *State Property*, when her phone rang. Looking at the caller id, it was Keisha. "What do you want, bitch?"

"Get out your feelings and come meet me and Red. It's important."

"Where?" Nicole said.

"My house."

Nicole hung up the phone and told her dude, "Bae, I'll be back!"

"Where are you going?" he asked.

"To meet Keisha and Red," she replied.

"Alright, be careful."

Nicole got in her car and she was driving down 79th street blasting her music.

I could've sworn I just saw Choc at the bus stop. Man, I know this ain't that bitch, Choc, catching the bus. Doesn't she know this is wartime? Let me turn back around and find out. I'll be damn, that is this bitch!

Nicole pulled out her gun.

Click! Clack!

She lowered her window down and let shots blast free as they hit Choc's body. Her body dropped to the ground instantly. Nicole pulled off and went straight to Keisha's house.

Damn, I forgot I gave her the key back. Nicole knocked on the door and Red let her in the house. Keisha was sitting on the chair in her room.

"What the fuck happened to y'all?" Nicole fussed.

They both told Nicole what happen and she couldn't believe her ears. "Damn, I'm glad y'all are ok. Man, so what's the next move?" "The next move is to get those bitches gone," Keisha said. "Hell yea. I want that bitch, Peaches, personally," Red said. "I saw that bitch Choc today at the bus stop. I shot that bitch up on sight. The look on her face when she saw me, it was like she knew she was about to meet death." "Really?" Keisha said. "Here she goes again, I hope this bitch don't get mad at me for killing this Choc bitch." Keisha walked up on Nicole and got in her face. "You know what? You're a bad bitch. Give me a hug." They were startled by a hard knock on the door. "Who is it?" Keisha yelled. "It's Smoke, open the door." "What the fuck is he doing here? Nobody told him to come here." Keisha flung her door open with a scowl on her face. "What the fuck do you want? Why are you at my house?" "This is what you wanted right?" Smoke asked. "Man look, I don't want shit to do with you. Wasn't you just talking to that girl and hugged up with her?" Keisha asked. "You're not paying me any attention though. I'm steady trying to get up with you, but you ain't replying back. What the fuck am I supposed to do? Wait for you, Keisha?" Smoke needed answers. "Smoke, you're a dog ass nigga and you need to leave." "I'm not going anywhere." Smoke grabbed Keisha, took her in the room, and pushed her on the bed. Nicole and Red just sat there in the living room. They vowed never to get in each other's business when it came down to relationship issues. Smoke pulled Keisha's pants off and licked her pussy. "This is what you want, right?" *Damn, as bad as I want to tell this nigga to get off me, I really need his dick right now.* Keisha turned over on her knees so that he could hit her doggy style. "Get this pussy, daddy," she cooed. Smoke pulled out his dick and made sure he pushed all his dick up in her. "Damn girl, I've missed this pussy."

Let me bounce this ass back because I think he forgot how this pussy rules him. Keisha bounced her ass and tightened her pussy muscles around his meaty dick. "

"Damn, you know how to work this pussy for daddy." He grabbed her ass and exploded off a big one inside her. They both stretched out on the bed, bodies sticky from sweat. Keisha kissed Smoke and they both laid there for a while relaxing.

"Red, I remember back in the day how everything used to be cool. We used to be at all the kickbacks fucking shit up, bitches used to be hating on us too hard," Nicole reminisced.

"Hell yea!" Red said.

"We need to throw something soon. Maybe chill for about a month because right now the streets are hot and you know the police be thirsty. Plus, I just murked that bitch Choc."

Somebody knocked on the door. "Damn bitch, it's a lot of pop-ups tonight." Nicole walked to the door asking, "Who is it?"

"Me, King!"

Nicole opened the door to allow in Keisha's uncle.

"Where the fuck is Keisha?" he asked.

"She's in the room sleep," Nicole told him.

"I haven't heard from nobody since that night. I just came over here to tell y'all that somebody just shot that bitch, Choc, and she's at the hospital fighting for her life. It's all over the news."

Nicole and Red looked at each other. "Awe shit, so y'all had something to do with that? Well, the police are looking for whoever shot her up so be ready. They're coming for y'all ass if she survives," King said as he left out the door. "Tell Keisha to call me. I'm still waiting on my money!"

"Man, what the fuck is really going on we need to lay low somewhere. Aye Keisha, come here now!"

"Damn bitch, why y'all yelling like it's the end of the world?" Keisha said, coming out of the back room. She had just hopped out of the shower when she heard loud voices.

"Man, King just came over here and said Choc's shooting is all over the news," Red spoke up for them both.

"So, what does that mean?" Keisha said.

Nicole was hesitant to tell her, so Red jump in. "Bitch, we need to leave. Choc ain't dead!"

Bitch, I'm not going no fucking where. That bitch ain't dead! Well, she will be even if I have to go up there and finish her off myself!" Keisha exclaimed.

"Yea bitch, then you'll be in jail washing big Bertha's panties while she's eating your cat," Red said.

"Listen, Keisha, we have to lay low for a while. We've been murkin' shit left and right. We are hot, G," Nicole said.

"I can't run from my city," Keisha exclaimed.

"Bitch, we are not running. We're just going on vacation," Nicole explained.

"I don't know y'all, me and Smoke just got back cool," Keisha hesitated.

"Keisha, I'm leaving before Choc rats us out. That bitch did see my face. This is crazy!" Nicole yelled.

"So, what's y'all plan? If I do leave with y'all, where are we going and what are we doing once we get there?"

"Man, we can go to New Orleans, Miami, Atlanta, some fucking where, but not here." Keisha just looked at them. "Man, y'all bitches are crazy. What happened to us? I thought we were riders."

"Keisha, we got to chill for a while let's do something fun for a change!" Nicole said.

"Ok cool. Where are we going?" Keisha asked.

"New Orleans first," Red blurted out.

"Don't get too comfortable when we leave either, bitch. We're coming back, hoe." Keisha looked at them like they were crazy.

"Damn, now I have to tell Smoke I'm leaving and we just made up. This should be easy I hope," Keisha said walking to her bedroom. "Hey baby, we need to talk."

"What's up, Keisha?"

"Baby, I got to leave for a couple of days. Shit's about to get real, and the girls and I can't get caught up here lacking, especially after Nicole failed at killing that bitch, Choc. The bitch is at the hospital and we know she's going to snitch whenever she gets a chance."

"Okay baby. Whatever you got to do, just don't leave a nigga hanging out here," Smoke stated.

"I promise baby. I won't."

Keisha started packing her stuff. She could feel Smoke watching her. "Baby, I'm coming back; I promise."

45

"You better and don't come back pregnant!"

"Nigga, if I come back pregnant, the baby is yours. Fuck you talking about."

"Come give me a kiss, lil girl," Smoke demanded.

"Baby, I wish you can go with me, but I know you got other shit to do," Keisha said while kissing him on the lips. "I love you, daddy!"

"I love you too, bae!"

"Nicole! Red! Are y'all ready? Let's go tear New Orleans down." They all left out the door excited for what lay ahead.

Smoke got up to leave, he was kind of mad that Keisha was leaving, but he played it cool. He wanted Choc to die. He decided to go up to the hospital where she was at to make sure she never woke up, but he wanted to wait until later on tonight.

Bang! Bang!

Smoke heard somebody knocking at the door.

"Who is it?" Smoke called out.

"Is my daughter here?" a woman's voice asked.

Smoke opened the door to see an older lady that resembled Keisha. He couldn't stop looking at her.

"Um, is she here or not? And who are you?" Keisha's mother asked.

"I'm Smoke, Keisha's boyfriend and she just left to go to New Orleans," he explained.

"New Orleans? What is she going out there for?"

"Ma'am, I don't know. Do you want me to call her so you can talk to her?" he inquired respectfully.

"No, it's fine. Just tell her that I stopped by."

"Damn she's mean as hell, just like her daughter. Let me call Keisha and tell her that her mom came here," Smoke spoke aloud.

Keisha picked up on the first ring. "What's up, baby?"

"Hey, your mom just left from over here."

"My Mom? What do you mean, Smoke? My mom? I haven't seen her in years. How does she know where I stay? Fuck! Uncle King and Uncle Richard must've told her ass," Keisha figured one of the two or even both let her mom know where she stayed. "Okay bae, I'll call you back."

Smoke didn't know anything about her family for real. Keisha's mom had been in prison for some years for beating Keisha's brother. She had come home drunk from the club one night and beat him because he wouldn't tell her where Keisha was. Keisha had been prostituting to keep money in her pockets. She had used that money to keep her and her brother in the latest gear because her mom was doing other stuff. Like getting high and partying.

Damn, this shit is crazy. Smoke grabbed his phone to call one of his guys so they can link up and discuss some business. His money had been looking funny since he came back on the scene, so he decided to turn up on niggas and fast.

Right when he was about to call Keith, Re Re sent a text to his phone.

Re Re: Nigga, when my brothers catch you, it's off with your head. I can't believe that you let yo bitch jump me.

This bitch got another thing coming if she thinks I'm worried about some lil niggas coming my way. I'll kill that bitch myself.

***

"Man, this is going be a long flight," Nicole yelled out. Keisha was in the zone, all she can think about is her mom doing a pop up after all these years. She was also thinking about what she was going to do with Smoke and how Choc was going to snitch on all of them. Her mind was going crazy.

"Bitch, my mama came to my house today after we left. Smoke called me and told me," Keisha said to her girls.

"What? Why?" Nicole asked, looking confused. "Your mom hasn't been around in some years! How is yo bro feeling about this?"

"I don't know. I haven't talked to him in a minute, but I'm going to call him when we touch down in New Orleans. She probably has already got in contact with him or probably not because that crazy ass nigga might put a bullet in her head. He's still hurt about what she did to him years ago, so it might not be no popping up at his crib."

"Yea because you know my boo is crazy." Nicole started laughing.

"Bitch, you still like my bro? You're a hoe," Keisha snickered.

"What the fuck are y'all talking about?" Red asked. "Oh, I can't know? It's cool. Fuck y'all bitches too."

Red didn't know too much about Keisha's mom, but Keisha was going to tell her when the time was right.

"Well, I texted hubby and he's mad as fuck that I left, but at the same time, he understands. I told him if I like it, we're moving to New Orleans or Atlanta." Red was ready to move anyways. This was the perfect opportunity to leave Illinois.

47

"Bitch, you know you ain't leaving Illinois, so stop playing with ya self," Nicole said matter-of-factly.

"Hell naw, that bitch ain't going nowhere. Dream big bitch, dream big." They all started laughing.

"What are we about to do when we get to New Orleans? I'm trying to get me, southern boy," Keisha said, dancing in her seat.

"Keisha, stop it. Smoke is gon' give you a southern ass whooping," Red said cracking up laughing.

"Bitches got jokes today, huh?" Keisha rolled her eyes and put on her headphones. She played Rich Homie Quan's "Bullet" and spaced out. Even though she was smiling on the outside, she was scared and nervous at the same time. She wasn't ready to face her mother considering she was the reason why her mom spent eight years in Logan Correctional Center. She snitched on her mother for what she did to her brother, so she knew her mom wasn't popping up to be nice to her. Her mom wanted revenge and she wasn't about to stop until she got it done.

chapter nine

They finally made it to New Orleans and checked into their room in the French Quarter. They wanted to get out and see the city. They'd heard about some place called the D Shop but didn't know what they were about to do or get into. They just knew that they wanted to have some fun. They had met these two niggas when they were walking down Bourbon Street in the French Quarter. Their names were Marv and Melvin and those southern accents were the truth.

Keisha felt as if she wasn't gon' get into too much because she wanted to stay faithful to Smoke, but them niggas made her pussy wet. They all got dress and went to the NOLA D Shop.

"Keisha, I haven't felt this good in months," Red said.

"Shit, me neither. Call them niggas and tell them to meet us in the front."

When they got downstairs, the niggas were right there looking so fucking sexy. Marv and Melvin looked like twins, but they weren't; they were just brothers. They were both in the latest designers and smelling good with fresh cuts.

"What's up, Shawty?" Marv said while licking them sexy ass lips.

"What's up and my name is Keisha, not shawty!" He couldn't stop looking at her ass. She had on some leggings and a T-Shirt with a nice pair of Nike Air Max 95s. Her hair was in a bun, she didn't want to be flashy. *Shit, I didn't know these niggas and I got my gun on me. I heard these niggas out here was some killers they won't get me.*

Nicole and Red were having the time of their lives smoking and drinking with the niggas. Keisha was just looking and observing her surroundings. They were serious about coming here to have fun. Keisha wanted to have fun too, but shit, if something pops off they couldn't all be turnt up. They finally got to the D Shop and that bitch was packed. These niggas were well known because bitches were mugging us and running up to these niggas like they were Lil Wayne and Baby.

I got my blunt and lit it I dome that bitch. "Aye turn up!" This bitch Red didn't give a fuck where we were at she was going to turn up anyway.

"What the fuck Keisha? Let's turn up! That's what we came up here for, remember," Red said, already feeling her buzz.

"Chill bitch, you're doing too much!" Keisha snapped.

"Bitch, I'm not doing enough!" Red screamed.

"Aye Nicole, Red is tweaking G. It's about to be some shit," Keisha spoke to Nicole, trying to keep her on point with Red.

I kid ya not, as soon as Keisha said that Red was over by the DJ booth arguing with a group of hoes.

"See what I mean, Nicole!" Keisha shouted over the music.

"Bitch, I'm from Chicago, you ain't on shit. I said excuse me for stepping on them beat up ass shoes," she heard Red yell.

One of the girls must have got tired of Red talking, so she swung on Red and missed. Red picked up a bottle and smashed it on the bitch's head. Bitches started coming from everywhere trying to jump on Red.

"Aw hell naw, ain't none of that!" Nicole yelled over the music. She ran over there slicing bitches up. Keisha fell in line and started beating bitches' asses. The police came and locked Nicole up for cutting one of the girl's face open.

"Damn, Red. Bitch, you got us hot up here. Now, Nicole is sitting in jail because she was helping yo ass," Keisha fussed.

"Bitch, them hoes was hating on us talking bout why we walk in there with them niggas," Red argued.

"Okay, so what we're about to do is check into another hotel because we don't want to chance them niggas bringing those bitches to the hotel and setting us up. Look at this vacation has gone wrong already."

Keisha and Red went back to the room, grabbed their shit, and jetted. It felt like someone was watching her.

"I'm leaving tomorrow, Red. After we bond Nicole out."

"Where are we going and why are we leaving?" Red asked.

"Red, something doesn't feel right. It feels like I'm being watched," Keisha began to explain. "I don't know what it is, but I feel so weird." When they finally check into another hotel room, she needed to get in the bath and call Smoke. It seemed like she couldn't shake drama. She was hoping that maybe he can help her feel better. Keisha picked up the phone to call Smoke and he answered on the first ring.

"What's up, baby girl?" Smoke spoke into the phone. He was happy to hear from her.

"Hey daddy. I miss you so much," Keisha cooed.

"I miss you too, ma!"

"Smoke, I want to come back so bad. I feel so uneasy here like somebody is watching me."

"Maybe it's because you're so used to ducking and dodging here. Just take it one day at a time and if you don't feel better in a couple more days, I'm coming to get you," he assured her.

"Okay daddy, I love you."

"I love you too, ma." They ended the call.

Keisha got out the tub and crawled into the bed. She couldn't sleep. All she did was think about the fact that she was ready for a change, but needed to make sure Choc and Peaches were off the streets. Red came and laid on the bed with her and talked her to sleep.

"Keisha, wake up. It's time to go get Nicole. Her bond is fifteen hundred to get out!" Red nudge Keisha.

"Okay Red, here I come. Give me ten minutes."

"This breeze feels so good, maybe we should walk," Red said as they walked out of the hotel.

"Bitch, I'm not about to walk nowhere. Did you forget about what happened last night? You're tripping," Keisha fussed, but she was serious as a heart attack. They got in the rental and drove to the New Orleans Police Department to get Nicole. When they pulled up in front of the building, Keisha stayed in the car while Red went in there to bond Nicole out. Keisha looked up and seen this lady walking out of the Police Department. *I wonder what a nicely dressed lady like that was doing coming out of there.* Keisha figured that she didn't work there because of what the woman was wearing. She looked like she was from Chicago. She got in this nice ass Mustang and her plates read; LOVELY!

51

chapter ten

"Isis, what the fuck are you doing in there? Get the fuck up now and clean up this house. You're a stupid bitch!" Isis' mom yelled from the other room. Isis got out of bed and just shook her head. *She always acted like this when she'd been drinking the night before,* Isis thought to herself.

"Here I come, mom!"

"Hurry the fuck up, you stupid bitch!" Isis' mom screamed again. Isis hurried out her room. "Isis, I'm tired of you, bitch. Bring your ass here now. You like talking back, right?" Isis' mom swung on her, busting her lip.

"Ma, I'm not doing anything. Please mom, no!"

"What have you been doing outside, being a hoe? Is that why you in here sleep all the time?"

"Mom no, I'm a virgin."

Isis' mom, Tamika, grabbed her hair and dragged her across the living room floor to the kitchen.

"Now wash my fucking dishes." Isis stood up over the sink and washed the dishes with tears flowing down her face. Tamika stopped liking her daughter when she started getting older because she reminded Tamika of a younger version of herself. "Isis, when you're done, go to the store and get me a pack of Newport's One Hundred," her mom demanded.

"Ok mom," Isis said. She finished washing the dishes, and when she was done she went to her room to get dressed. Isis put on her jogging pants and t-shirt with her white Nike's. "Mom, I'm ready," Isis whispered to her mom.

"Go get the money off my dresser and hurry ya ass back. Don't be out there talking to none of these niggas either."

"Yes, ma'am," Isis said.

"And bring me a Swisher!" Isis mom yelled while Isis was walking out the door. Isis decided to go to the store on the corner of her house on 61st and in King Drive.

"Aye shawty, come here." Isis turned around to see one of the local corner boys walking towards her. She instantly froze up, as he continued to walk up to her. He said, "What's up, shawty? What's your name?"

"I'm Isis and what is your name?" Isis said shyly.

"I'm Country. Why are you looking so down?" Country asked.

"My mom and I got into it, no biggie." Isis was kind of happy that someone took interest in her because she wasn't getting any love at home from her mom.

"Oh, is that right?" Country said standing there sizing Isis up. Country was a short, handsome dark skin dude. He liked young girls because he felt like he could run over them. People always said that he reminded them of Lil Wayne. Country was born in Chicago but spent most of his childhood in Atlanta, where he picked up his accent. When he came back to Chicago all the girls use to say to him, 'boy you, Country' and that's how he ended up with the nickname Country.

"Well, check this out. Put my number in your phone."

"Sorry, I don't have one," Isis said quietly.

"Okay, then meet me up here in a few hours. I want to get to know you better."

"I'll try," Isis said. Isis went to the store to get her mom's cigarettes thinking to herself, *how am I going to be able to pull this shit off.* Isis was a very pretty girl with no street smarts, but little did she know, she was about to be introduced to the streets quicker than she expected. Country walked back to the corner where his homies were standing in front of phat boys' corner store. "Man, did you see shawty? I need to make her my girl."

"Country, don't you already have three baby mammas?" Smiley said with confusion written all over his face. He and Smiley had been friends their whole life, Country called Smiley his right-hand man.

"Look, man, I got this. You're worried about the wrong shit. I can't wait until she meets me in a few hours. I'm going to see where her head at literally, nigga," Country said to Smiley.

"Boy, do you know who that girl's mama is? Her fucking mama is crazy as hell man. She be beating on her and everything. The last thing lil mama need is a nigga like you fucking her head up more than it already is."

"Man, you sound like a hater right now. You're mad cause a nigga trying to get his dick sucked or you got a thang for shawty too?"

Smiley just looked. He had more than just a thing for her; he wanted to get to her before Country did.

"Come on, nigga. Let's go upstairs to bag up the rest of this dope."

Smiley was thinking hard about what Country had planned for Isis. He didn't like that one bit; he needed to get to her first. He didn't want Country to get too attached because that would've messed up his plans. *Damn nigga, snap out of it.*

Isis walked back in the house and her mom was asleep on the couch. Isis took the bottle of liquor out of her mom's hand, covered her up with a blanket, and kissed her mom on the jaw. No matter how Isis' mom treated her, she loved her mom to death. Isis went to her room and started thinking about Country. She was wondering if he could be her Prince Charming or just another nigga like her daddy, whoever that was. Her mom said she was raped, that's why Isis didn't know her dad. She laid across her bed looking off into space.

I guess I'll take a quick nap and try to go out to see Country later. I'm tired of being cooped up in this house. Isis fell asleep daydreaming.

Bang! Bang!

Isis was waking up by someone banging on the door, whoever it was at the door was now in the house. Isis heard her mom screaming, "No, please no. I'm sorry. Please don't hurt me!"

Isis ran in her closet crying. She couldn't believe what was happening. She heard a man's voice say, "Bitch, I told you that I would find your nasty ass," followed by gunshots. After the gunshots, things went silent.

Isis stayed in the closet. She was so afraid to go out to see what was going on. A couple minutes later she heard sirens and footsteps. "It's the police. Is anyone here?" Isis heard someone call out.

Isis came out the closet. "Yes, it's me. Is my mom okay?" she asked.

"No, I'm sorry honey. Your mom is dead," the office notified her. Isis was confused. She really didn't know what to do; she didn't know how to feel. She didn't see a body when she walked in the living room, just a lot of blood.

"Why did it have to be my mom?" Isis asked herself. *It's all my fault. I should've never been a problem in her life. What am I supposed to do without a mom or dad?* Isis left out the house because she couldn't bear being in there alone without the presence of her mom. *She used to be so good to me. I don't know what went wrong over the years. I remember when my mom was so full of life.*

Isis had no one to call. It has always been her and her mom. Isis started crying. *Where am I supposed to go?* She took a walk to clear her mind and she noticed Country sitting outside. She walked up to him, her eyes bloodshot red from crying.

"Hey Country."

Country looked up at Isis and said, "What's up?"

She just started crying. "Ma, what's wrong?"

Isis looked at Country and said, "Somebody just murdered my mom." Country didn't know what to say. He just got up and gave her a hug to let her know that everything would be okay.

Isis continued to talk to him. "What am I going to do? I have nobody; my mom was all I had. I'm lost. My world is gone, so maybe I should just die."

"No Isis, you can come to my house until we figure things out. Let me clear a few things up with the guys and make a phone call before I go." Isis just stood there waiting for him to make sure everything was cool before he left. Country walked back up to Isis and said, "Come on, my car is in the back." Country drove an all-white G6 with black tints on his windows. He opened up the door for Isis and they drove off down the street until they made it to the highway. The drive was long and quiet.

Isis took her hair out of the ponytail and let her natural hair hang down her back. Country couldn't help but watch her. he was very amazed at Isis' beauty. He thought to himself, *how he can show her a different part of life.* They finally pulled up to a big brick house. There was an all-black Benz in front of it. They walked into the house and a Marvin Gaye song was playing. The smell of soul food filled the air. The living room was furnished with all-white furniture and a flat screen was mounted on the wall. There were three glass lion sculptures in different parts of the living room.

"Mama, where are you at!" Country yelled out.

"I'm here baby."

Isis just stood there with her head down. "Hey son, how are you?" Country's mom greeted him. After giving him a kiss on his jaw, she looked over to Isis and said, "Hey baby, Kevin called me and told me you were coming. I'll take good care of you. Are you hungry?" his mom asked.

"No, I'm ok. I just want to lay down," Isis meekly responded.

"Ok, you can go in the front and lay down until I get the guest room together for you."

"Thanks," Isis said. She walked into the living room and stretches out on the couch and started daydreaming.

"Boy, what are you gon' do with that girl? You already got Tasha, Ki Ki, and Quita," his mom fussed.

"Mom, I'm just trying help to her."

Country's mom just looked at him and said, "Um," and walked off. Country went to the front and sat next to Isis. He rolled up his weed and turned on the TV to watch videos.

Isis sat up and asked Country, "Can you hold me?"

He wrapped his arms around her and she cried herself to sleep. When Isis woke up, it was twelve in the afternoon. Country was gone by then and she didn't want to get up, but she had to use the bathroom. Isis waited a moment then got up and walked towards the bathroom.

The smell of bacon filled the air and the song, "Let's Get It On" was playing by Marvin Gaye. Isis thought to herself, *Man, this lady must love him.* She went to the bathroom and there was bath water already in the tub. There was a pair of Rock and Republic jeans and a black fitted shirt with a brand-new bra, panties, and fresh socks with a letter.

Dear Isis,

Isis, I can't imagine what you are going through and I just want to be there for you the best way I know how. I see something in you that I don't see any anybody else. You are very special inside and out, you just have to learn how to embrace it. If you need anything, mama will take care of you. Try to get to know her; she's pretty cool.

Sincerely,

Your future, Country.

chapter eleven

Isis put the letter down and got in the tub to relax her mind. she drifted into deep thoughts thinking about the good and bad things her mom did to her with tears flowing down her face. Isis placed a hot face towel on her face. *Man, I have to go back to my house. I have to kill the person responsible for this.* Isis washed up with some Love Spell body wash. *This feels so good. I just want to stay in this bathroom forever.*
Knock! Knock!
"Isis, are you okay in there?" Country's mama asked from the other side of the door.
"Yes, ma'am."
"Okay. I cooked breakfast. Make sure you come downstairs to eat," Country's mama said and walked off.
She got out the tub and walked in the room. Isis was only seventeen, but her body was perfect. She had curves to kill for, just enough up top with ample booty. She was shaped like Delicious from the reality TV show with Flava Flav. She looked in the mirror and said, "I have to get it together for my mama."
She put her hair in a ponytail, cleaned the bathroom, and went to the kitchen to eat breakfast. Isis didn't notice how big the kitchen was last night. Isis sat at the kitchen table, said her prayers, and then ate breakfast.
Mama came in the kitchen, touched Isis' shoulder, and said, "Isis, are you okay?"

57

"Just a little bit," Isis said. "I just need to go back home for a couple of days."

"Honey, are you sure that will be okay?"

"I don't know yet, but it's a lot of things I need to figure out because things are not adding up to me. My mom was young and murdered; I'm just trying to figure out why."

"Baby, I will pray for you and when and if you need anything, don't you hesitate to come back here. Okay?"

"Yes, ma'am."

"Chile, you don't have to call me ma'am. I'm mama now."

Isis just looked at her. Isis finally got Country to drop her off at her apartment. He was kind of hesitant to do that, but Isis wanted to go back home to clean it up and just try to make sense of it all.

When she stepped foot in the door all type of different emotions took over her. She stayed in one spot for a while and just inhaled the air. The smell of death filled the air. "Mom, what did you do?" Isis started to clean up and she heard a knock on the door.

What the fuck maybe it's the killer returning.

"Who is it?" No response. Isis grabbed a knife and walk to the door. She peeped out the peephole and it was the dude she'd seen with Country when she first met him. "Hi, can I help you?"

"Yes, you can." He kicked the door open, grabbed Isis by the hair, and put a gun to her head. "Drop the knife, bitch. Now!"

"Please no, don't hurt me."

"Bitch, yo mama owed me! Now open up them legs and let me get some of that sweet tight pussy." Smiley ripped at her clothes. He tore her shirt off and sucked her breast.

Isis was crying, "Please no. Stop!"

He tried to unbutton her pants, but Isis punched him across the head. She was going blow for blow with him. She wasn't backing down for anything. Smiley saw that Isis was a fighter, so he picked her up by her throat.

"Either you're going to let me get this virgin pussy, or I'm going to take it and then I'll blow your brains out next." Isis tried her best to get him off her to the point where she couldn't fight anymore and her screams became muffled.

He finally got her pants off, so he shoved his big dick in Isis. With every pump, Isis felt the pain, but she couldn't even cry. Her emotions were very numb at this point. Smiley kept abusing Isis' vagina until he came inside of her. He stood up, buckled his pants, spit on her, and left. Isis laid there crying. She tried getting up off the floor and her legs were weak. She crawled to the bathroom, held the doorknob to help lift herself up, and it felt like all her insides left her body. Blood was running down her legs and she didn't know what to do. Isis looked at herself in the mirror and didn't see the same person she'd seen before; she just didn't know her reflection in the mirror. She didn't feel like herself. *I don't know what to do.* Isis didn't want to go to the hospital. She took a long hot shower. Her body was badly bruised, it hurt to move. No matter how hard Isis tried to clean herself, she still felt very nasty. Isis got out the shower, went to her mom's room, and curled up in her bed. Isis didn't get any sleep. She tossed and turned all night crying and hurting from the worst experience she had ever gone through.

Isis wanted to go to the hospital, but at this point, she didn't trust anybody. Isis decided to get up, so she went through her mom's stuff with more tears flowing down her face. *Mom, why did you leave me here alone?* Isis thought to herself. She stumbled across a box sitting in her mom's closet. She picked up the box, moved it from the closet, and sat down on the floor. Isis couldn't stop crying. She opened the box and there was a nine-millimeter pistol that was all black, one hundred thousand dollars in cash and a diary. On the front of the diary, it said, "A letter to my daughter." Isis was stuck. The tears stopped, the first page she read said,

Dear Daughter,

If you are reading this it's probably because I'm in jail or dead, whichever one it may be, stay strong and don't drop another tear for me. Not saying I'm not worth your tears, but because now it's time for you to be strong and cold!

Chills ran down Isis body.

I know that I've been hard on you and that's only because I never knew how to be a mom, so I gave it to you hard only because I didn't want you to fuck up your life. I did a lot of shit, baby. A whole lot... So from this day forward, I want you to follow my instructions.

Isis thought to herself, *even in death she's still controlling me,* as a smile crept across her face. The letter continued.

With some of the money, buy a nice car. I know that you still remember how to drive, right? Remember the times I took you test-driving? That's because I was preparing you for your new life. Put the rest of the money up in a stash for later. The gun, yes, the gun, keep it on you at all times. You'll need it. Remember don't trust anybody. There are no friends in this game we're about to play. Now, under my bed, I have a key tapped to the bed rail. It's a key to a safe deposit box at the Bank of America, box number three zero three. There you will see that I left the deed to your brand-new house and your house keys. Please leave that shack. I had your new house built from the ground and that house is in Country Club Hills. You will love it. It's a five-bedroom house with three baths and it's already furnished with everything you may desire. It's gated for your protection and your name is in big gold letters, ISIS, on the gate. You don't need a nigga for shit. I repeat, for shit. Don't trust them or tell them your business. When you get your car, go straight to the house, then you read the next page and it will tell you what to do next.
P.S. If I'm a dead, don't bury me. My only wish is that you get me cremated.

Isis just sat there stunned. She couldn't even think straight. *What's going on?* Isis thought to herself. *I guess it time for me to put myself in a woman position.* Isis got up and went to her bedroom, put on a pair of jeans, a white t-shirt, and a pair of tennis shoes. She got her duffle bag out of the closet and packed a few items to remember her mom. She grabbed the money, diary, the key and she tucked the gun into her jeans.

She got some lighter fluid and a match setting their house on fire. Isis walked off with not a care in the world. The whole walk felt so good, it felt like she was about to live a different life. The sun was starting to come out as Isis walked all the way to the bank to go check the safe deposit box. It was still early when Isis got to the bank, so she decided to go sit in Starbucks because the bank wasn't open yet. She walked to the counter and ordered a tea. The waiter at the counter said, "You're cute."

Isis said, "Thanks."

She gave the waiter a hundred-dollar bill and said, "Keep the change." Isis set down and zoned out while looking out the window off into space. Somebody walked up on Isis.

"Excuse me, miss," an unknown voice startled her. Isis jumped up into defense mode. "What's up? I saw you over here looking good and I just wanted to say hi," the stranger said.

"I'm not really in the mood, sir. I had a fucked-up night, so if you'll excuse me." Isis brushed the man off and walked back to the bank to get her life out of the safe deposit box. Isis walked into the bank and at the front desk, there was a heavyset black woman.

"How may I help you?" She had a southern accent, Isis always knew how to talk to people.

"Yes, I'm here to check my deposit box," she explained to the woman.

"Okay, can I see your ID and what's the box number?"

"Three, zero, three," Isis said with confidence. The lady looked at Isis as if she was studying her. Isis got irritated. "Okay, can I leave now?"

"Oh yes, sure. Go ahead. Go straight down that hall and you will see a room with all the deposit boxes. Search until you find your number."

Isis rolled her eyes, as she walks off she can feel someone watching her. Isis turns around to see if she can see who it was, but no one was there. Isis grabbed her stuff and left the bank quicker then she came. Isis caught a cab to the car lot where she purchased a jazz-blue 2016 Dodge Charger SXT Sedan with black Interior, fully equipped. She paid thirty thousand dollars for it in cash.

She got in her car and turned her radio to the news station. She heard the breaking news update. The headline was about her mom's house.

"Hi, my name is Amber Crews and I'm live from ABC News. The house of the murdered victim, Tamika Lewis was burned down this morning and it's believed that her seventeen-year-old daughter, Isis, was inside the home. Anybody that has any information about this horrific crime, please contact the Chicago's Police Department."

Isis smiled and thought to herself now I can live a different life she put her address in the GPS system and drove to her new home. Isis pulled up to her house and she couldn't believe her eyes she put her code in the gate and the gate swung open. She parked in front of her house, stuck the key in the door, and walked in. She couldn't believe her eyes.

"Oh, my goodness! Look at this! What am I going to do with all this room, mom?" she spoke to her mom's spirit.

It was well furnished and everything was well put together. Isis was ecstatic. She didn't want to look at any more of the house; Isis just wanted to read the next page of her mom's letter. Isis opened up the diary and begun reading.

Dear Daughter,

When I wrote this note to you, I felt all types of different emotions knowing that I'm not going to be around you for a while or I'm not going to be around for you at all. I need you to go in the basement; there you will see many of my secrets. I will let you know your next step after that. Don't worry; don't be scared to go in the basement. You're safe here.

Isis looked at the diary and said, "You have got to be kidding me," but followed her mom's instructions. She went into the basement and she couldn't believe her eyes. The basement contained one hundred bricks of heroin and on every brick, a smiley face logo was branded all over them.

chapter twelve

Country stood in front of Isis' old house that was now ashes. He and Smiley were talking.

"Man, I don't what happened with Shawty. I dropped her off and she was safe. I should have never left her, man. What the fuck was I thinking? She didn't deserve to die. Shawty could've had so much potential," Country lamented.

"It'll be alright, bro," Smiley attempted to comfort him.

"Man, I wanted to make a future with her. I mean at first I didn't, but when I saw how much shit she was going through I wanted to give her a new chance at life."

"Well, she's gone now, man. It's time to move on."

As they walked off Country felt someone watching him. "Smiley, it feels like I'm being watched, man."

"It's probably your guardian angel," Smiley said trying to be sarcastic. Country just looked at him.

Isis pulled off and thought to herself, *mama said don't trust anybody. These niggas tried to set me up.* Isis went to purchase her a phone. She needed some company. When Isis got home, she called her friend Lah Lah.

Lah Lah was a girl that Isis met at school and she was Isis only friend. Isis really didn't know too much about Lah Lah. She just knew that she needed a friend because she was by herself. Lah Lah always used to come to Isis' house, but Tamika would tell her to stay away from Isis.

Isis didn't care; she wasn't going to let her mom run Lah Lah away, so she'd sneak her in sometimes when her mom was gone or sleeping. The phone rang four times and as soon as Isis was about to hang up, someone answered the phone.

"Hello," Lah Lah said on the other end. Isis didn't say anything. "Who is this?" Lah Lah yelled.

"It's me, Isis."

"Who the fuck is this playing? Isis is dead!" Lah Lah was getting pissed with the games.

"Lah Lah, it's really me. I'm not dead. Please, I'm scared being by myself."

"Where are you?"

"I can't say right now. Can I come get you?" Isis asked.

"Yea," Lah Lah said.

"Meet me at our spot, Lah."

Isis and Lah Lah were two of a kind. The only difference is Lah Lah was street smart and Isis was book smart. Isis pulled up at the park where she and Lah Lah used to meet up. Lah Lah was there looking confused and smoking on a blunt. Isis called her phone.

"Come on. I'm in this car right here," Isis told her.

Lah Lah kept her blade in her mouth. She walked to the car, opened the door and to her surprise, Isis was in the car. She started crying. "Bitch, I thought you were dead."

The whole ride back to the house, Isis told Lah Lah everything. Isis pulled up to her gate, typed the code in, and parked in front of her house. Lah Lah was stunned.

"Isis, your mom left you with all this? Pinch me bitch, I'm dreaming," Isis said.

"Pinch me too, I'm still trying to wake it." They walked in the house Lah Lah stares at everything as if she was in a movie.

"Bitch, can I stay?" Lah asked.

Isis said, "Yea bitch, I need you more than you'll ever know."

Lah Lah pulled out her blunt asking, "Can I smoke in here?"

"Yea girl, go ahead. Matter of fact, let me get some too." They both started laughing. Isis was just about to hit Lah Lah with some more info, but she thought against it for now. Isis got up and went to the basement to make sure the door was locked. She came back upstairs to find Lah Lah was up there in her panties and bra getting high out of her mind. She passed Isis the blunt; she puffs it and started choking. She hit it a couple of more times like a pro. Isis was high as hell.

Lah Lah played some music and started playfully dancing on Isis. That shit kind of turned Isis on and at first Isis was a little confused by those feelings. Lil Wayne's song started playing. "Long as my bitches love me," Isis sang and grabbed Lah Lah's ass.

Lah Lah turned around and said, "Do you want some of this?" Isis just looked at her. Lah Lah kissed Isis in the mouth, and then she took Isis pants off then started eating Isis' pussy like it was fruit. She looked up at Isis and told her, "I'm gon make you mine." Isis sat back and let her do what made her feel better.

This shit sholl feel better than what I encountered with that nigga Smiley, she thought. Isis started shaking and creaming all over Lah Lah's face. "OMG, I don't know what's happening but this shit feels good." Lah Lah caught all of Isis juices.

"It's about to be me and you against the world baby," Isis said while rubbing her fingers through Lah Lah's hair. The rest of the night they smoked and planned on how they were going to kill Smiley and Country.

***

Country was a real smart street nigga and something wasn't adding up with this whole Isis being dead story, so he called his mom to let her know what was going on. His mama told him that she'd get in touch with his Uncle Benny, the head investigator on the Police Force, to see if they actually found a body in Isis' house. Country's mama got in contact with her brother and asked him a million questions until he finally confessed that there wasn't a body found. When Country's mom broke the news to him, all type of emotions took over him. "What the fuck happened? Where did you go?" Country asked himself. He picked up the phone to call Smiley. Smiley picked up on the first ring.

"Man, you would never believe what I found out."

Smiley said, "What nigga?"

"Man, it's Isis. She ain't dead." The call ended.

Country looked at the phone and said to himself, "I know this nigga didn't hang up." Country called Smiley's phone again and no answer. Country sat back in the chair and started thinking. He called his hit man, Murder. "Murder, man, I need you to kill that nigga Smiley and

65

find my girl Isis. I don't know what is going on, but I feel like Smiley did something to her."

***

Isis waited on Lah Lah to go to sleep, so she can read the next note in her mom's diary.

I know you're wondering what type of shit I was into, but mama was a true hustler. I never let it show because I didn't want the FEDs at my door. Smiley was a lil nigga that I use to fuck on until he gave me an STD. I fell completely back from him and I sent your uncles to rob him. I thought I was in the clear until he caught me selling his shit around the hood. He told me he'd kill me or even have one of his police friends put me in jail for the rest of my life if I didn't give him his shit back. Isis, it's very important that you get that nigga back for what he did to me. I got the perfect plan. Our next move will be our best move. Chin up, baby. You'll need your gun and move in silence.

Never ever let your left hand know what your right hand is doing. You may need a friend with you. Use them to help you and then kill them.

Isis set there with a crooked smile on her face ready for war. She got up and laid down with Lah Lah. She kissed her on the cheek and said, "Get up." Lah Lah sat up.

"So… I want to torture those niggas. I just need to get close to them without making a sound."

"Well bitch, we need to talk about this another time because I'm tired right now." Lah Lah laid back down, but Isis stayed up a little while longer until she fell asleep right under Lah Lah.

chapter thirteen

Country drove around the whole city trying to see if he saw Isis anywhere he was confused about everything that was happening. If I see Smiley before Murder does, I just might kill him myself. Country phones ring it was Mama.
"Hey mama, what's up?"
"Son, come over to the house now. I've got somebody that I need you to meet."
"Okay," Country replied.
"Come now!" she demanded.
"I'm on my way," Country said on the other end of the phone. He rushed to his mom's house. "Anytime she called me to meet with someone, it's always about something that can help me out in the future," Country said aloud. When Country got in the house, it was a man sitting in the living room. This was the same man that bumped into Isis in Starbucks.
Country looked confused at his mama asking, "What's going on?"
"Have a seat, baby. This nice man has something that he wants to share with you." Country's mom had a lot of connections in every hood before she became a church member. Everybody loved mama, she kept her eyes and ears in the streets simply because her son was in them. Country looked at the man and said. "What's up?" and shook the man's hand. My name is Ed. I'm from around the way. I'd seen Isis at Starbucks the very next day after the fire and I started following her after that. Her mom used to come to the club and fuck me all the time

for a few bucks. The whole time she was fucking me, she was plotting to set me up. She and Smiley robbed me for a few pounds and right after that, she is killed. I was following her daughter because I wanted her dead, but first, I needed to find out where my shit was. I followed her to this nice ass house out there in the suburbs and the only thing that is protecting her was that big ass gate with her name on it. I still wanted to kill her until your mom called me asking me about her and out of respect for your mom, I'll give Isis a pass. I just need your help getting my shit back."

Country sat there and started laughing. "Yea, okay. I got you, old school."

Country couldn't believe it. *This girl is still alive. I can't wait to see her. Man, this shit is beyond crazy.*

"So, when do you want to do this?" Country asked.

Ed replied, "Tonight."

***

Smiley was sitting back in deep thought. He couldn't believe that Isis was still alive. He picked up his phone to call his sister Lah Lah.

Lah Lah answered, "What's up bro?"

"Sis, have you heard from yo lil friend, Isis?"

"Why would I hear from a dead person? And why are you asking about her anyway?" Lah asked.

"Look Lah, she's not dead. If you hear from her, I need you to call me ASAP. Her mom ran off with my shit and I think she got it."

"Okay, bro. I got you of course," she said hanging up the phone. Lah Lah wasn't about to tell her brother anything. she had her own plans for Isis.

Isis walked in on Lah Lah asking, "Who are you talking to?" Lah Lah jumped.

"Isis, you scared me. I was talking to my brother," she explained.

"Who is your brother?" Isis asked out of curiosity because she never knew Lah Lah had a brother. That's when it dawned on her; she didn't know anything about Lah Lah. Then she started thinking to herself, *I'm going to have to kill this bitch.* "Okay cool. Come in here and watch a movie with me. After that, we're going to the city to find Country and Smiley."

Isis wasn't really ready to go kill them; she just wanted to see Lah Lah's reaction. Lah Lah's face dropped.

She said, "No, let's just stay here. We're not ready."

"Damn bitch, how ready should we be? It's either kill or be killed."

"Isis, we're not ready. These niggas will have our heads," Lah continued to argue her point. That's when Isis realized that Lah Lah knew more than what she expected.

Country and Ed decided to ride out that night. The whole ride Country was quiet, but Ed, on the other hand, couldn't stop running his mouth. Country wanted to kill this nigga bad, but he thought twice. He had to get to Isis. They finally pulled up a half block from Isis' house and they waited for a little while to see if she would come outside. Country got tired of waiting, he pulled out his nine-millimeter with the silencer on it and blew Ed's brains out. He got out the car and called Murder. "I'm here, find Smiley and trunk that nigga."

Country found a way through the gate and he rang the doorbell. Lah Lah and Isis jumped up out of their seats wondering who even knew where she was. Isis pulled out her pistol and without thinking blew Lah Lah's brains out. Country on the other side of the door didn't know what to think. He thought Smiley was in there, so he started kicking the door until the door opened. Isis was standing there with fire in her eyes. She put the gun to his head and said, "I will blow your fucking brains out."

Country stood there trying to plead his case, "Please Isis, I love you. I would never ever hurt you."

"I saw you talking to him," Isis said to Country. "You were talking to Smiley. You dropped me off that night just so he could rape me," she screamed.

"Listen Isis, we need to go. The police will be here in a minute."

"The police? Do you think I give a fuck about the police? Huh, Country?" Isis put the gun to her head.

"My life ain't shit, Country. I really thought you liked me, but you didn't," Isis said sadly.

Country dropped a tear. "Listen Isis, don't do it. Please don't do it."

Country's phone rang and it was Murder.

"Aye man, I can't find that nigga nowhere," Murder went on to explain.

Bang!

A loud gunshot went off and came through the house. Silence filled the room. Someone shot through Isis' window. Isis jumped and Country grabbed her. "I got you, baby. You can trust me."

69

Bang!

Another gunshot they didn't know what to do.

Isis laid there with her pistol clutched, ready to go to war. She stood up, walked to the door with her gun ready and already aiming. A soft voice finally spoke, "Isis, don't kill me."

"Mom, is that you? I thought you were dead. What's going on?"

"We can talk about that later. Grab yo shit and let's go," her mother tried to get it together. Isis locked eyes with Country.

"Mom, what the fuck? I'm tired of going through this shit with you! I thought you were dead and you were just trying to kill me. Drop the fucking gun, mom."

Country sat back looking shocked. He couldn't believe this was Isis' mom, the infamous Tamika. His mom had run-ins with Tamika before in the past.

Isis looked at Country. "Get that key off the counter, go to the basement and get all the dope," she instructed him. Tamika started screaming but before she could tell her daughter not to trust Country, Isis let the rest of the clips out in Tamika's chest. She didn't know that was the biggest mistake of her life.

Isis sat in her hotel smoking blunts back to back. Country was just looking at her. He couldn't believe the way she was looking. Isis was different now. She was rougher, not that innocent Isis that she once was before. Country had seen this look on a lot of chicks in the hood before when they let the streets get the best of them. Country touched Isis' hand and she jumped away from him.

"Isis, you can trust me. I need you to slow down on the blunts so we can talk. You need to think rationally. You just murdered your mom. We need to focus on how we're going to get out of this hotel and state." Isis just looked at him. "Can I trust you? I don't think I can, Country."

Country just looked at her. "All I can do is give you my word, baby girl. Let me lead you. You're not ready for the streets."

Isis just looked at him and started crying. "This isn't for me. My mom and Smiley destroyed me."

Country was pissed to even hear his name. Country wiped her tears away. "Lay down and get some rest." Isis went to sleep on Country's leg.

The next morning Isis woke up in Country's arms. She pushed Country's arm. "Wake up," she urged him.

He got up stretching. "Yea Isis," Country said.

"I'm ready to leave. I always wanted to go to New Orleans. Can we go there to live?"

Country wasn't really ready to leave, but for Isis, he would. "Yea ma, let me book our flight." Isis just looked at him with a glow in her eyes. They left the hotel room and got on their plane to New Orleans.

"Bye Chicago," Isis said. Country had everything figured out; he didn't want Isis to lift a finger when they got to New Orleans. He had already booked their room at The Ritz-Carlton Hotel until they could find them a place and settled in.

Country had arranged for one of his buddies to go over to Isis' house to clean up the bodies and to bring the heroin to New Orleans, but until then, he wanted to take her to get pampered, out to eat and to the show. Isis was still very tired from the traveling. She just wanted to rest, but to show Country her appreciation she got up and got dress.

Country's phone rang and he answered after the second ring. "What up, Murder? What's going on?"

"Man, that nigga Smiley went ghost. Nobody has heard from him," Murder stated.

"I'll talk about that when I get back, I have to make sure that my shawty is straight," Country told him.

Isis walked out the bathroom with a white robe on, her skin was smooth, and her hair was naturally curly. Her body looked so good in that robe and it made Country's dick hard as a rock. Isis walked up to Country, kissed him and said, "Thanks for everything."

"No problem, baby girl. Let's get dressed. I got something else planned for you."

chapter fourteen

Country sat there waiting on Isis to get done. While he was waiting, he called Murder to see what was up with everything back home. Murder picked up his phone on the first ring.

"Aye man, how are things looking down there?" Country asked.

"Yeah, everything is cool, just trying to lay low."

"Okay. Have you heard from Smiley?" Country asked.

"Naw man, I haven't heard from him or seen him," Murder lied.

"Hey baby, that was so relaxing," Isis said to Country.

Let me call you back man Country hung up the phone. Isis thought that was suspicious but she didn't say anything she didn't want to spoil the moment.

Country's phone rang again it was his baby mama, Quita. He sent her to voicemail. Isis and Country went to the movies to see *Perfect Guy*. Throughout the whole movie, Country was thinking about his conversation with Murder. *Man, something ain't right with that nigga Murder. That nigga's whole conversation was off. I'm not feeling that nigga anymore. I have to go to Chicago for a day to see what's up.*

Isis could feel that something wasn't right with Country. "Hey baby, are you ok?" she asked.

"Yeah, I just have a lot on my mind," Country replied to Isis.

Quita screamed out, "Let me go! You don't have to do me like this. I don't know where he's at I have not heard from him. Please don't hurt me," Quita yelled again. "I have a baby! Please don't kill me." Shots rang out and Quita's body dropped. Smiley shot her in the face. *Bitch should've told me where that nigga was hiding.*

Isis and Country left the show he had five missed calls and voicemails he checked his voice mail and the first one he heard was going to change his life.

Isis sat in her room listening to Kelly Rowland's "Ice" while smoking a blunt and thinking about her life. *Man, I'm still young going through so much pain. I don't know who to trust or what to do. I'm trying to give a fuck about Country, but he's been pushing me away for a few days now. He's been acting really out of character to the point it makes me wonder if I should have offed him instead of my mom,* Isis thought to herself. She walked to the window and picked up her mom's diary. *I wonder what the fuck she had planned for me next.*

***

Dear Daughter,

It's gonna be a time in your life where you need to turn your back on me and everybody else. I'm not happy about the way I treated you, but at the end of the day, I don't feel sorry for shit I did. I only made you a monster for what's next. Good luck dealing with the world and the people in it. They never had love for us, so what makes you think they will now?

Isis took a long puff off her loud blunt. *Damn, how do I deal with this shit? I just killed my mom on some not thinking shit. My feelings of being raped and beat on are constantly playing a big part of my life and I'm just ready to get my revenge back on whoever I think had something to do with it.* Isis left out the door to go take a walk and her phone rang. Isis picked up her phone. It was a private call.

"Hello?"

"Bitch, when I find you, you're dead! Dead!" a man's voice yelled into the phone.

Isis response was, "I'm already dead."

That call had Isis on charge. Country was nowhere to be found, so she didn't even want to leave out now. "I have too much going on in my life. I can't fuck with Country like that, but since he knows too much I'll keep him around. I need to know when my dope gets here because I'm ready to set up shop in all the hoods out here and be the biggest female drug dealer in New Orleans. I need to get to Magnolia Projects. From all the songs that I heard on the radio, I know I can set up shop over there. I know the niggas will love my Chicago ass," Isis chuckled. *I see it's a lot of drug dealers in New Orleans, but I'm going to change the game. My dope is supposed to be here tomorrow. Let me get some rest so I can network in the morning.* Country walked in and laid next to Isis.

"Where have you been Country? You've been gone all day," Isis asked.

"Baby girl, I've been handling business. I got a lot of shit going on right now. I hope you understand."

"Yeah, I guess, but you have been kind of standoffish lately."

"I know, but I want to do everything to make it up to you, plus I got some good news. We're going to be making moves soon." Isis just looked at him unimpressed. She had her own plans; some involved Country and some didn't.

Country was the type of nigga that didn't know how to show his emotions. He wanted to tell Isis what was going on, but being a man, he chose not to. That could have been his worst mistake. The next morning the sun was glaring through the window. Isis got up, rolled a blunt and made breakfast for her and Country. They both sat at the table to eat breakfast and it was an awkward silence. Isis started the conversation off, "Well, I was thinking about going to do a little shopping today to pick up a few things."

Country stopped her in her tracks. "Well, I got something to show you first. Get dressed."

Isis just looked at him. *I guess he's trying to make up for not showing me any attention. Let's see what he has up his sleeve now.* She went in the other part of the hotel room where the bedroom was located and her clothes were laid out on the bed. "Oh my God, he did it again." Country got Isis an outfit from Pink. It was a pink and gray sweatsuit with a pair of all white Air Max Zeros. There was a gift box laid on the bed that housed a Cartier watch with pink diamonds embedded in it and the matching earrings.

Isis wanted to trust Country, but she couldn't find it in her heart to do so. Isis got dressed, flat ironed her hair, put her Mac lip-gloss on, and walked into the kitchen where Country was sitting. He couldn't believe his eyes. He'd never had a girl that looked that as good as Isis looked. She looked so pure and innocent. All Country wanted to do was make Isis happy. He stood up and kissed Isis on the lips. As bad as he wanted to fuck her, he held back. Being a gentleman to her is all that he could have done. Isis and Country got in the cab. He handed Isis a blindfold. Isis looked at him confusingly.

"Nigga, what do you want me to do with that? I'm not putting that on." They both started laughing.

"Shawty, you're good with me. You have nothing to worry about when it comes to us. Now, put them on." Isis put on the blindfold in the ride and it felt like forever before suddenly they came to a stop. He took the blindfold off her face. What she saw in front of her brought tears to her eyes.

chapter fifteen

Tears fell down Isis face; she was confused on so many levels. She didn't know what to say.

"Oh my God, Country! You shouldn't have." Country had outdone himself with this one. Isis' emotions were running wild looking at her new home. It was the Melrose Mansion they once used it for wedding venues. Country felt like Isis could use that space for a new home, so he bought it for her. It was ten bedrooms, five bathrooms, with a clear glass pool in the backyard. She had a very spacious walk-in kitchen with a diamond chandelier hanging from the ceiling, white marble floors throughout the whole mansion and every room were furnished. Isis couldn't believe her eyes. There was a painting of Isis on one of the bedroom walls. Isis was filled with so much joy. She wanted to hate Country, but the way he treated her took her mind away from all the stuff she been going through.

Isis turned around and said, "Thank you. I love it," as she kissed him. "Country, what can I do to repay you? You're being way too nice to me and I don't deserve this." Isis grabbed his hand and took him upstairs. She pushed him on the bed and started to unzip his pants. Country grabbed Isis' hand and told her to stop. She looked at him like he was crazy and began sucking his dick. Country's moans became intense; he didn't know she had it in her. She then got undressed and laid on the bed. Country put one of her breast in his mouth and sucked her nipples. He then took his tongue and licked down her stomach. He went all the way down and start licking her pussy and it tasted so good to him. Her juices were sweet. He put his tongue in her hole.

Isis felt so much pleasure; she couldn't believe that it felt so good. She started shaking uncontrollably. She was embarrassed because she didn't know what that was making her shake like that, but she didn't hold back. Country got on top and stuck the head of his dick in her pussy. He couldn't believe how tight her pussy was and he instantly knew that he was going to be with her forever. Isis dug her nails into his back and they both moaned from pleasure. They slept the whole day away.

Country woke up in the middle of the night to call his mom. He wanted Isis to be looked after while he was gone to Chicago. His mom didn't answer. He called again and no answer. He went in the room with Isis and told her that he needed to go to Chicago and check on his mom.

"What do you mean?" Isis said.

"Look, like I told you before I have a lot going on out there. My mom is out there and not answering her phone so I am really worried."

"Country, what do you have going on that I can't know about? Maybe I can help you."

"Look, just promise me that you can trust me because it's too much for me to tell you right now."

"I guess Country," Isis said while rolling back over.

"I guess that's all he wanted now he's leaving like everybody else," Isis cried with tears rolling down her face. Country kissed her and walked off. "Country, please come back."

"Baby, I promise that I'll be back."

Country still had not told Isis about his baby mama. He has not told Isis anything about his life. "Don't forget the package will be here in the morning. Make sure you'll be looking out. I have a safe in our master bedroom. Call me when it comes."

Isis got up the next morning. She cooked her breakfast, smoked a blunt and waited for the package to come. She got another call from a private number, but she didn't answer.

"Man, I don't know why they keep calling me private. I don't know what I did in this world to deserve all of this." Isis was startled by the doorbell ringing. "Who is it?" Isis said.

"John. Country sent me."

She grabbed her gun off the counter thinking about what happened to her the last time. She didn't want to take another risk. She opened the door and it was a big black dude that looked like he worked on cars. "What's up?" John said.

"Hello!" Isis had her nine-millimeter in her pocket just in case John wanted to be murdered. "You can take it to the basement." Isis couldn't keep still; she was worried that John would try something with her. When John was done, she paid him and he left. Isis called Country to let him know that everything was cool. Country picked up the phone and told Isis that he'd be home in two days and she was cool with that because that gave her enough time to devise a plan.

Isis got dress and went to the Magnolia Projects. She sat outside on a stump and watched everybody and everything from the corner boys crack heads, thots, and the neighborhood kids. People had their grills going, two kids were fighting over a bike and it was a couple arguing right next to Isis. She was enjoying the scenery. Isis rolled up a blunt and as soon as she was about to light it some girl sat next to her. The girl was a Lil Kim look alike, but a more ghetto version. She was tatted all over. She spoke to Isis, "Hey girl. What are you doing around here? you don't look familiar."

"I don't look familiar cause I ain't from around here," Isis told her.

"Well, this not the place for a newbie like yourself. By the way where you from? My name is Cream and I'm from right here. Anything you need to know, ask me."

"I'm Isis and I'm from Chiraq." Isis looked at her and didn't respond it was something about Cream that Isis liked.

"So, what are you doing out here?"

"I'm thinking about moving here," Isis told her.

"Girl, here out of all the other places you could have gone. Why here?"

"Man, I don't even know. I just needed a different type of experience in my life. Here, you want to hit the blunt?" Isis offered.

Isis watched Cream closely. It was something about her that was a little odd, but for the most part, she was cool. Isis wanted to give her a chance.

"So Cream, where do you work at? I need a job."

"Girl, I dance and do a couple of other things on the side. You can come work with me if you want to," Cream proposed.

"I don't know. I'll figure something out." Isis jumped when her phone rang. "Hello!"

"Yeah bitch, I'm going to get you," a male voice said on the other end. Isis hung up and decided to call Country. Country's phone rang three times and went to voicemail. She decided to call his mom's phone, but the lines were busy. *What the fuck?* Isis thought. She called Country again, this time it went straight to voicemail, so she left him a message. "Baby, when you get this please call me. I'm worried."

"Sorry about that Cream. Can you show me around? Tell me everything about your city. I need to know because right now, I'm here to stay. This is the life down here I don't think I ever wanna leave. Look at the scenery, I never really seen shit like this before."

Cream looked at Isis like she was crazy.

"Girl, what do you mean? This not shit compared to the club scene." Cream took Isis upstairs to her apartment. It was kind of small. Her kitchen was red and black; her furniture in the living room was all white with gold picture frames with pictures of Cream at different clubs. Her bathroom was laid out with pink and purple decor. Her bedroom set was gold and white and there was a stripper pole in the middle of her room. Cream's apartment was nice, considering she was living in the projects. "Isis, you want something to drink?" Cream asked.

"Yeah, a cup of water will work." Isis pulled out her phone again and called Country when a girl picked up the phone.

Country's first stop was his mom's house. When he got there the house was quiet. He pulled out his gun, went upstairs to find his mom laying in her bed.

"Mom! Mom!" Country touched his mom. "Are you ok?"

Country's mom rolled over and said, "Baby, what are you doing here?"

"Mom, why aren't you answering your phone? I've been calling," Country said.

"I took those sleeping pills baby, you know how that is."

"Mom, I need you to come with me. Pack your stuff because it's too much going on and I need you to watch over Isis while I come back here for a little while. Just pack a little stuff to hold you over."

His mom looked at him and said, "Chile, I'm not leaving my house."

"Mom, they killed Quita and I don't know where Lil Kevin is at. I need you to get dressed now and come to New Orleans with me."

Country's mom stood there for a minute. She didn't drop a tear. she shook her head and started packing. Country and his momma left and as they were pulling off, Country's other baby momma, Tasha, came out the closet. She heard a phone ringing. She looked on the bed and noticed that Country left his phone. The name on the phone said 'Wifey'.

"Hello?" The other line went dead and Tasha started laughing.

Isis went home she was so angry that she started throwing dishes around; she couldn't believe Country's lying ass. She tried to call again and the same female started laughing on the phone. Isis said, "Bitch, when I find out who you are I'm going to kill you and tell Country he's dead too bitch." Isis went in her front room, sat on her couch, rolled up a blunt and started thinking about Country. *I can't believe this nigga betrayed me saying that he was going home to check on his mom, but he's with another bitch. I can't wait until he gets back here. I am seriously going to hurt him because my feelings are not to be played with; they've been played with enough. I need some company and I need some company right now. I will call Cream, but I really can't trust her right now. Oh, I can't wait until Country walks in the door. Let me go get this diary. I should burn it. She's another motherfucker that pretended very well and you see what happened to her.* Isis opened up the diary and started to read it.

Dear Daughter,

I remember when I was younger and I had my first boyfriend. It was hard for me to trust because all that I had been through. I hope you don't have that issue growing up. I know that I've been a fucked-up parent and I was raised by a fucked-up parent. I don't know where I'm at right now, dead or alive, but just know I loved you the best way I knew how. Remember every page will be a piece of me.

Sincerely,

Tamika

Isis tossed the diary under the bed. It's like she knew what Isis is going through. Every time she managed to hit a roadblock, there was sound advice in the diary. She went to her dresser to get her blunt. When she heard the doorknob turn, Isis grabbed her gun, cocked it back, and aimed straight at the door. It was Country and his mom.

Country was staring down at the barrel of the gun. "What the fuck is wrong with you? Put that shit away."

"What the fuck is wrong with me? What the fuck is wrong with you? Why the fuck is you even here?" Isis yelled.

This was the only time that Country's mom was a little afraid because the Isis that left her house that day was not the same Isis standing in front of her. this Isis had the death look in her eyes.

"Baby, calm down." Country's mom said.

Isis sized her up and gave Country's mom a look that would've cut deep if it was a knife. She turned back to Country asking, "So are you here for me or you trying to fuck me over?" She put the gun to his head.

"Isis put the gun down," Country said.

"I'm not putting anything down. I called your phone and a bitch answered. Country, you said that you loved me." Isis turned the gun on herself.

"I lost my phone. Isis, I will never hurt you. Call my phone, baby. Call it now. I think that I dropped it somewhere," Country was trying to explain to Isis. However, Isis was not trying to hear that shit. She turned the gun back to Country.

"Leave me alone and don't come near me." Isis grabbed her car keys and left out the house. She called Cream, and Cream picked up on the first ring.

"Can I please come over?" Isis asked.

"Yea girl come on. Is everything ok?"

"No, my boyfriend and I got into it. I need some air."

chapter sixteen

Isis gets to Cream's house in a few short minutes. It didn't take her too
long to get back to Nolia.
"Girl, are you okay?" Cream asked Isis.
"Yeah, I'm straight. I just needed to get out the house."
"Girl, it looks like you have had a rough night."
"No, just so stressed out. I got a lot going on in my life," Isis said.
"Well, you want to drink?" Cream asked.
"No, I don't drink. I just smoke."
"Well girl, roll that shit up then. Let's go in here and dance." Cream
grabbed Isis' hand and led her to her bedroom. Cream played that song
by Jacques, "Persian Rugs" and got on the pole, doing all type of tricks.
Isis was in awe watching Cream dance.
She took a puff of her loud again, Cream had on a thong and bra. She
had so many tattoos. Isis was kind of turned on by Cream's body and
Cream knew it. She walked up on Isis and tried to twerk on her, but Isis
jumped up.
"I'm cool. Don't do that." She passed Cream the loud blunt and left. "I'll
text you in the morning." Cream was stuck looking dumb.
Isis walked to her car and some nigga grabbed her arm. He looked like
the grim reaper with Golds in his mouth.
"What's up, Shawty?"
Isis was scared as hell, but she didn't let it show. She snatched her arm
away from him and looked him up and down. "Can you please not
touch my arm ever again?" then she walked off and got in her car. She

just didn't know that she just met her worst nightmare. Isis checked her phone. She had a text from Country.

Bae: *You are about to lose the best thing that ever happened to you.*

***

Smiley knew his sister was probably dead. They couldn't find her or her body anywhere and for that reason, Country's baby mama had to die.

"Man, shut your ass up before I kill you like I killed your mama."

"I want my daddy," Little Kevin said.

"Aye, tie this lil nigga up and duct tape his mouth. Put him in the other room while you're at it. I can't wait until I find this nigga so I can torture this nigga like I'm about to do his fucking son." Smiley started laughing.

Tasha walked in and said, "Smiley, I couldn't kill his mama. The nigga walked in as soon as I was about slit her fucking throat. I do have some info for you. He went to New Orleans with his mom to be with the bitch Isis and I got his phone."

Smiley couldn't believe Tasha was really telling on her baby daddy.

"You must really hate that nigga." Smiley looked at Tasha. Tasha was Country's first baby mama. She thought that she was going to have a future with him, but he did her dirty by fucking her over. Country had sex with Tasha's sister, Quita, and had a baby by her. Tasha wasn't going to quit until Country was dead.

Tasha and Smiley went in the other room. Tasha laid across the bed.

"So, what are we going to do with that boy?"

"I don't know yet. Maybe we can just kill him," Tasha said.

"Aye, you are one cold-hearted ass bitch," Smiley said.

"First of all, she should have never been fucking my nigga and had a bastard ass baby by him. Hell yea, I'm a cold-hearted nigga. I want to blow that lil nigga's brains out."

"Shawty, calm down," Murder said while walking into the room.

Tasha's eyes grew bigger. Just the sight of this crazy looking nigga sent chills through her entire body.

"I gotta go," Tasha said.

"What are you leaving for? We still have some unfinished business to take care of, so sit down and relax," Smiley said.

"Okay, I need a drink," Tasha said as she lit up the blunt. "I need to relax my mind." She laid across the bed and Smiley handed her a shot.

Tasha gulped the shot of Cîroc that he handed her. The blunt in rotation and another shot, all three of them sat there getting drunk and high. Tasha grabbed Smiley's dick and started sucking it. Murder was sitting on the chair in the corner watching everything. Country's phone started ringing. Tasha grabbed the phone and saw that the name on the phone read Wifey. Instead of Tasha pressing the end button, she answered the call. Isis couldn't believe what she was hearing. She walked into the house with the phone on speaker.

***

Country was sitting on the couch, so Isis handed him the phone. She looked at Country and said sorry. Country listened to call and he heard his baby mama, Tasha's, voice. "Ooh Smiley, you like this pussy?" "Yea baby, this shit is good."

"Murder, you want some?" and that's when the call ended. Isis just stood there looking at Country. He couldn't believe what he just heard. Isis rubbed his head. "Don't touch me, Isis. Don't fucking touch me," he lashed.

"Country, I'm sorry. I didn't know. This is all new to me," Isis whined.

"I'm tired of telling you to trust me, Isis. You keep pushing me away. I told you that I was going through a lot of shit!" Isis grabbed his hand.

"Baby, I'm sorry. Please, I want to go through this with you. I love you, baby." Country just sat there with his head down and he started telling Isis everything...

"I had three baby mamas. One just got killed by Smiley, the other one is fucking Smiley and my man's, Murder, has linked up with the nigga, Smiley. Also, my son, Lil Kevin, gotta be with the nigga Smiley too." He looked up at her. "You still want to fuck with me or not? Either way it goes, I have to go back and get my sons and make sure my other baby momma gets out of Chicago with our daughter." Isis stood there looking at him with so much remorse in her eyes.

"Baby, why didn't you tell me that you had kids in the beginning? I would've never stop fucking with you because of that. I want to be there for you like you were for me." Country couldn't believe what Isis was saying.

Country's mom was standing their ease dropping. "Baby, I'm so sorry about how I talked to your mom. I promise in the morning I will beg for her forgiveness. Give me a kiss Country."

Country hit Isis with a pillow. "Stop playing Country. Give me a kiss." Isis jumped on him and kissed him on his lips. His dick instantly got hard. As much as Country wanted to be mad at Isis, he couldn't resist her.

They went in the room Country laid on the bed and told Isis to sit on his face Isis took her clothes off and sat on Country face just like he asked this time she didn't take anything as a surprise she rode his face like it was a dick he couldn't believe how good her pussy taste. She came all over Country's face.

She unzipped his pants, taking charge as she rode his dick from the back. Her pussy was so wet. Country grabbed her ass cheeks. He was about to cum, so Isis tightened her pussy muscles on Country's fat dick. "Ohhhhh baby, I'm about to cum." Isis started bouncing on his dick harder. He grabbed her ass even tighter. Isis jumped off his dick and slurped up all of his nut. Country was shaking uncontrollably.

"Damn girl!" Country yelled.

Isis just looked up him and said, "Do you forgive me, daddy?"

"Yes, baby. I do."

Isis woke up at six that morning. She walked into the guest room where Country's mama was sleeping. She laid across the bed and tapped her leg.

"Mama," she whispered.

"Yes, baby."

"Can we talk?" Isis asked.

"Yes, baby. What's up?" Mama replied.

"First, I want to say I apologize for yesterday. I've been through so many things with so many different people that I get very defensive when I feel like I'm being hurt. I'm not making any excuses for my actions; I just wanted to give you some insight on why I lashed out like I did. I love your son with everything I have left in me. He has shown me something different in life and I just want to let you know that I will never ever disrespect you again."

Mama just laid there staring at Isis for a long time before she started talking. "I don't appreciate how you treated me yesterday. I felt like I walked into the devil's pit, but when you left out Country told me some of what you've been through so I understand. Not only that, it takes a lot for someone to apologize for what they have done, so I accept your apology. Just don't let it happen again," Mama schooled her.

"Okay," Isis said shyly.

"Now get over here and give me a hug, girl." Isis gave mama a hug and walked into the kitchen to prepare breakfast. She made bacon, eggs, rice, and toast with cold orange juice. Country came into the kitchen and slapped Isis on the ass.

"Good morning, love."

"Good morning, daddy." They both smiled thinking about last night.

"Country, how do you think your baby mama got your phone?"

"I don't know. The only place I went to is my mom's crib. Fuck, that bitch followed me!"

***

Tasha went to the basement where Lil Kevin was. She snatched the tape off his mouth.

"Aunt T, Aunt T, are you here to save me?" Tasha smacked him in the mouth.

"Don't call me that and no I'm not here to save you, you little bastard!" Tasha was dark skinned and very skinny. Her hair was all over her head, clothes dirty and with three days of food stains and drink stains on them.

"I hate you little boy and I'm glad your mama is dead."

Lil Kevin started crying, "But I didn't do anything. Aunt T, please help me. I need water."

Tasha grabbed the knife and cut Lil Kevin across the face. He started to scream. Tasha spit on him and taped his mouth back together.

She walked up the stairs to find Smiley sitting up there on the couch, playing with his gun and talking to Murder. "So, this is what we're going to do next. We are going to have Tasha get in contact with that nigga, Country. Make him feel sorry for her, so he can come up here to rescue her. When he gets here, we kill him and then you can go find that lil bitch, Isis," Smiley said while rubbing Murder's thigh, and then they kissed.

Tasha couldn't believe what she just saw. Tasha went to the bathroom and started throwing up. She couldn't believe what she just saw. Tasha had to pull herself together because she didn't want Smiley to know that she knew he was gay. Tasha called Smiley to the bathroom. "Smiley!"

"What girl?"

"I need a towel. I think that drink got me sick."

87

He came into the bathroom where she was to bring her a towel to wipe off. "Look, I need you to get in contact with yo baby daddy."
"How am I supposed to do that? I got his phone, remember?"
"Tasha, it seems like you're backing out. What, you scared now?"
"Nah nigga, I'm not scared. I'll try to call his mom." Smiley handed Tasha the phone and she called Country's mom. The phone rang a couple times before she answered.
Mama picked up. "Hello?"
Tasha didn't say anything.
"Hello?" Mama asked again, getting irritated.
"Hello, Mama. Are you around Country?"
"Who is this?"
"This Tasha."
Mama rolled her eyes and handed the phone to Country.
"Yooooo!"
"Hey Country. I need you," Tasha said.
"What's up? Does my son need something?"
"No. Can u please help me? I'm scared. I can't find Lil Kevin and Quita is dead."
Country remained calm. "I'll be out there tomorrow. Meet me at your place."
"Ok Country, I'm sorry about everything." Country just looked at the phone and hung up.
"Baby, who was that?"
"It was that bitch, Tasha. Get ready. We have to be in Chicago early tomorrow," he explained.

***

Smiley and Tasha were laying in the bed. Smiley started talking about what he was going to do to Country. Tasha couldn't get it out her mind that Smiley was gay. *Man, what the fuck? I thought I could have had a chance with this nigga. He got me setting up my baby daddy and shit,* Tasha thought.
"Aye, you listening?" Smiley asked.
"Yea, I'm listening, nigga," Tasha lied.
"So, when he gets out here tell him that you know where Lil Kevin is and bring him back here. That's when we will kill him," Smiley explained the plan.
"Smiley, you think this a good idea?"

"Bitch, you act like you still want to fuck with this nigga or something," Smiley said.

"It's not even like that. I just know that we have to plan wisely fucking with him," Tasha said.

"Look, I'm about to go to the store. When I come back you better be thinking straight." Smiley left out the door. Tasha got up and started cleaning and drinking. She was so nervous that she wanted to leave the house, but her selfishness wouldn't allow her. She wanted Lil Kevin and Country dead.

Bang! Bang! Bang!

Tasha jumped up. "This nigga must have left his keys again," Tasha said, walking towards the door. "Who is it?"

A male voice on the other side of the door said, "Me, open the door."

"I knew this nigga left his key." Tasha opened the door and to her surprise, she was face to face with death looking down at the barrel. The man on the other side of the door said, "Open your mouth." Tasha sat there in shock. She didn't move and sweat started dripping down her face. The gunman shoved the gun in Tasha's mouth and said, "Bye bitch," and blew Tasha's brains out.

The gunman looked all around for Lil Kevin until he found him. He grabbed Lil Kevin, jumped in his car, and drove off.

When Smiley got there, he couldn't believe his eyes. "What the fuck?" Smiley yelled. He ran straight to the basement and saw that Lil Kevin was gone. He called Murder and got no answer. He looked around the house for Country's phone and it was gone. He heard police sirens and left the house.

Shit, what the fuck happened? I need to lay low for a couple of days. Smiley pulled off and went to his other spot that no one knew about. He called Murder's phone again and Murder picked up the phone.

"What's up?" Murder answered.

"Man, where are you at? Somebody killed Tasha and took Lil Kevin. Meet me the corner of 51st and South Lawndale. This shit is crazy," Smiley said.

"I'm on my way now." As soon as they hung up the phone, Smiley's phone vibrated. He picked up and seen a text with the news headline. "Little boy has been dropped off in front of the University of Chicago Hospital. The little boy is in critical condition. Identity has not yet been confirmed. Any information, please call the Chicago Police Department."

Smiley was stuck he didn't know what he was going to do. All his plans were shattered. *Man, I got to get the fuck out of here before Country gets back. Tasha was trying to tell me that this nigga, Country, wasn't anything to be played with.* Smiley was so deep in thought that he didn't realize he was being followed by his worst nightmare.

chapter seventeen

Isis tossed and turned all night. She couldn't sleep. She sent a text to Cream and they chatted for a while. She went to the kitchen to get a glass of water.

Mama was sitting at the kitchen table when she saw Isis come into the kitchen. She told whomever she was talking to that she'd call them back. "Hey, mama. Are you okay?"

"Yes, baby, I'm okay. Just worried about my grandbabies is all."

"Who were you on the phone with?" Isis asked, looking at mama and waiting for an answer.

"Sit down, Isis. This is going to be a long story." Mama typed on the phone, searching for the Chicago News and the story about Lil Kevin was on there. Isis couldn't believe what she was reading. When she was done, she gave Mama her phone back.

"Now listen Isis, I was a part of the mob back in the day, and I can make anything happen without lifting a finger. I don't want anything to happen to you and my son, so I handled the big shit for you. I got somebody following Smiley, so when y'all get there it will be an easy catch. That's if he doesn't notice he's being watched." Isis took a drink of her water and she just started laughing. Mama was looking at Isis like she was crazy. "Girl, what's funny?"

"Mama, you're cold. I can't wait to put a slug in Smiley's head. I really want to make him suffer like he'd done to me."

"Whatever you do, Isis, come back safe. What I need you to do is tell Country that Lil Kevin is in the hospital in critical condition."

"Okay, Mama," Isis said. Isis turned around because mama called her name.

"Y'all watch out for Murder. He's slick," she warned. "I couldn't track him down."

"Okay, Mama. I got this from here." Isis left and went to wake Country up, but when she got back in the room Country was gone. She looked everywhere in the house and she couldn't find him anywhere.

"Mama! Ma! Mama, Country is gone!" Isis screamed.

***

Country was already on the plane on his way to Chicago. Country felt so bad for leaving Isis. He didn't want her to get hurt. He knew Isis was going to be mad at him, but that was a chance he decided to take. The plane had finally landed at the O'Hare Airport.

When Country stepped off the plane, he felt like a new man. He called his baby mama, Ki Ki, and told her to meet him at the Marriott along with their Daughter Kionna.

"Boy, what's going on? Why are you rushing me to leave? I don't have shit to do with her fucking ass."

"Get up and do what I said. If you want to die, stay right motherfucking there and I will be to get my motherfucking daughter. Now, what is it gonna be?" Ki Ki hung up the phone.

"This stupid ass bitch!" Country yelled. Country got in his rental and went to Ki Ki's house. Isis was blowing up Country's trap phone and he was not answering.

***

"Oh my God, I can't believe he left without me." Mama was on the phone talking to her hit man letting him know about the stunt Country pulled. Isis left out the door and went to Cream's house. She knocked on the door and no answer. Isis walked in and Cream was in the shower with the music on listening to Lil Wayne's "Sorry for the Wait."

Isis walked into the bathroom and pulled the shower curtain back. Cream almost jumped out of her skin she was so scared she through some soap at Isis.

"Bitch, you're crazy."

"Stop lacking bitch, you want to take a trip with me?" Isis asked.

"Hell yea. Where are we going?"

"Chicago and it's not your normal trip, so are you in or out?"

"Bitch, I'm in!" Cream screamed.

***

Country pulled up to Ki Ki building on 64th and Lowe Street to the brown building. When he got out the car, shots were fired.

Isis was in deep thought when she heard her phone ring.

"Hello Country, is that you?"

"Yea baby, I just got shot at."

"Where are you at baby?" Isis asked full of concern.

"I'm in Chicago."

"I know you're there, but where?"

"I was going to get my daughter from Ki Ki's house and some nigga walked up on me talking about he knows me. When I turned my back on the nigga, he started shooting at me. Man, I ain't ever seen this nigga before and to think about it, he had a New Orleans accent."

"Damn bae," Isis said.

"Isis, I think I'm being followed. What I don't understand is why the fuck would a nigga from New Orleans be following me," Country said.

"Bae, I don't know but I'm on my way to you now."

"Isis please be careful and watch your surroundings. We don't know about these New Orleans motherfuckers." Isis cut her eyes at Cream.

"Okay bae, I'm on my way. Bye." They ended their call.

How am I supposed to explain to Country the reason why I got this bitch Cream with me? Think, Isis think. Cream and Isis was just boarding the plane. Isis didn't want to break Cream heart; she was so excited about visiting Chicago. *I need to let her know something.*

"Hey, what was that phone call about?" Cream asked.

"I have to go alone. Maybe we can do this next time? I have way too many personal problems to deal with right now. Here, take this, and go shopping." Cream counted the money and it was five hundred dollars.

"Bitch, you don't have to give me this." Cream tried to hand the money back to Isis.

"Bitch, keep it. I'll be back soon," Isis said.

Cream never had a friend like Isis. All of her friends were slum buckets. Cream wanted to keep Isis around longer. Isis finally got seated on the plane and Cream was still standing there looking sad. Isis put her headphones in and let her music take control of her brain. *Man, I need a loud blunt right now,* Isis thought to herself. Isis fell asleep. She woke to the pilot saying, "We are now about to land." Isis felt like she had to throw up. Her stomach was boiling. Just the thought of being in Chicago brought back so many horrible memories. She sent a text to Country to let him know that they were landing.

Bae: *Okay bae. I'll have a driver out there waiting for you.*

Bae: *Oh yea, don't make any moves. I have something to tell you.*

chapter eighteen

Isis was waiting out at the O'Hare Airport for ten minutes. The smell of cigarettes and that Chicago air, she didn't miss a bit. "Omg, where is this driver?" Isis said.

"Excuse me, miss. How are you today? Are you Isis?"

Isis looked at him confused. "Who are you?"

"I'm your driver, Mr. Black. Country sent me." Mr. Black held his hand out to shake Isis' hand. Isis put her index finger up to pause this interaction.

"Hold up." She called Country to see if Mr. Black was cool.

"Yea, he's straight ma," Country replied.

Isis shook Mr. Black's hand and said, "Where's the car?"

Mr. Black walked off towards the car and Isis followed him.

He opened up the door and Isis couldn't believe her eyes. It was an all-white stretch limo with cream leather interior. It had TV's built in the seats, and a bar full of liquor. Isis didn't drink, but she needed something right now so she poured herself a shot of Cîroc. She sipped it first. "Ugh, this is very nasty." She sat the glass down. Isis sent a text to Country.

Bae: *Where is he taking me? This ride seems to be taking forever*

***

Murder met Smiley on 51st Street. They both went to Smiley's hideout house. Smiley was so scared; he didn't know what to do. "Man, where the fuck was you at? I think Country is out here, man. You need to find him," Smiley said.

Murder looked at Smiley and said, "Nigga, I know you're not scared?" As soon as Smiley was about to open his mouth to respond, gunshots rang out tearing the doors off his house. They both scattered around the house trying to hide and then they heard a car speeding off down the street. Murder ran to the door to see who was out there.

"Smiley! Smiley!"

"Come here joe!" Smiley ran to the door and seen his sister's head laying on the ground with a dick in her mouth and a note that said, "I've got yo your daddy, nigga. You wanted to play, so let's play. Tell yo sister to take your daddy's dick out her mouth." Smiley started throwing up. "It's gon be okay, man. I'm gon handle this for you," but deep down inside Murder was really scared. He'd never seen any shit like this in his life. He knew that he had to call Country and set Smiley up.

"Murder, what are we going to do?" Smiley asked.

"Shit, I don't know. This just made me sick as hell," Murder said.

"I need to find my mom. I need to find her now. What the fuck did I just do?" Smiley started crying.

"Man, we need to get the fuck out of here," as soon as Murder said that a police car was pulling up. The police sirens weren't on and that was a sign of a bad cop, especially after shots were fired. The cop walked up asking questions.

"I was called out because of shots fired."

Smiley knew that was bullshit. They were in a secluded area, so no one was around to call the police.

"Everything is fine, sir," Murder said. They had already hidden Lah Lah's head.

"Well, I see the door is shot out. I'm going to have to take you down to the police station for questioning," the police officer said.

"What the fuck for?" Murder yelled out.

The police handcuffed the both of them and that's when a woman walked in the door. Smiley's face dropped.

"You dirty bitch!" he yelled.

The woman started laughing.

***

Isis had finally made it to Country and she jumped into his arms.

"Baby, are you okay?" Isis screamed. "Baby, why would you leave? I could have helped you. Are you fine?"

97

"Yes, baby. I'm okay," Country said. "The bullet just grazed a nigga."
"Baby, what's going on? I've never had to deal with anything like this
before. I'm scared, but I'm not scared if that makes sense. I'm down to
ride for you, but you have to trust me. I don't feel like I can trust you,
Country, if you just up and leave. I love you," Isis said.
Country couldn't believe what he was hearing. *This girl is really falling
for me,* Country thought.
"Listen baby, there's no time to get scared. It's either kill or be killed
and we are not getting killed. We have to keep our eyes open at all
times. It's about to get real. I still don't know where my baby mom is at
and I don't know where my daughter is. That stupid ass bitch ran off
and she's not answering her phone or anything."
"Where does your baby mama live? I need the exact address because I
need to get there to get your daughter. I will find her. You don't even
have to come; you can stay here because we don't have to bring your
baby mama. We can just take your daughter because, at the end of the
day, we have to make sure that your baby is safe. I know that I forgot to
tell you something. You might want to see now."
Country sat down so he could listen to what Isis had to tell him. "Okay,
so I don't want you to snap once I tell you everything. I know that you
wanted to handle things on your own, but your mom did a few things
for you," Isis started to explain.
Country shook his head. "I told her to stay out of my shit. I wanted to
do this by myself. I don't need her to do everything all the time. She
acts like I'm a baby." Country picked up his phone to call his mom and
air her ass out.
"Baby, you might not want to do that yet, there's more," Isis said.
Country put his head down in his hand. "Go ahead Isis, finish."
"Well, your mom sent a hitman to wherever Smiley was hiding. When
the hitman got there, Smiley was nowhere to be found. he shot your
baby mama, Tasha in the mouth and he rescued Lil Kevin. Look, he is
in critical condition at the University of Chicago Children Unit. All we
have to do is make sure your baby is straight, so we can take him back
to New Orleans and kill them niggas."
Country just looked down he couldn't believe what he heard. He
grabbed the phone to call his mom, but she didn't answer. He called
their house phone and she didn't answer. "Man, what the fuck? Why the
fuck is she not answering her phone? This the shit I be talking about."

Isis walked towards Country. "Maybe you should just try to calm down so when we leave out this house, we can have our minds right. You said it's either kill or be killed, right? So, what you need to do is lift your head up, so we can do what we came here to do and go home." Country stood up, looked at Isis and said, "I knew you had it in you. Now, let's go."

Smiley couldn't believe it. *I thought this bitch was on my side,* Smiley thought to himself.

Murder was looking scared and more scared by the minute. "I hope you don't think he's going to get away with this shit, bitch," Smiley said from the back of the patrol car. "You think you can just kidnap me, bitch, and get away with it? I'll have motherfuckers at your head. We can do this the easy way or we could do this the hard way. Just like you have people watching me, I have people watching you too.

"Did you really think that I was going to be on your side over my baby daddy? Nigga, you got to be tripping. Either you pay me to let you go or you're a dead man," Ki Ki said from the front seat looking back at Smiley. Ki Ki started laughing.

"So, you really want to play? I like this," Smiley said.

"Pull over!" Ki Ki yelled again. "Pull this motherfucker over now." Officer Benny pulled over. Officer Benny had been fucking Ki Ki for years and Kionna is really his daughter. They didn't want Country to find out, so they kept it a secret.

Officer Benny pulled over and Ki Ki Jumped out the car. She grabbed her gun and opened up the back door. "Listen, bitch ass nigga. I don't need your threats and motherfucking lies. I know damn well your gay ass ain't been following me. You've been too busy fucking Murder in the ass." Ki Ki started laughing. "Oh, you didn't know I knew that right?"

"Bitch, I got cameras all over your house, so before you speak again," Ki Ki shoved her gun down Smiley's throat. "Enjoy this motherfucking ride because only God knows when you'll take another." She pointed the gun at Murder. "You want to suck it too, bitch?" Murder just put his head down.

Isis felt sick. She'd been feeling this way for the past couple days. Isis had been throwing up, having night sweats and weird cravings. She didn't know what was going on. Isis and Country were on their way to the car and Isis fell out on the ground. Country dropped to his knees.

"Baby, get up. What's going on? Somebody help me!" Country screamed out. There were people were watching and some were calling the police calling for help.

The ambulance finally got there and Isis was just regaining consciousness.

"Country, what's going on?"

"Bae, you just fell out. Have you eaten anything?" he asked, full of concern.

"Not today, but I have been feeling kind of sick lately," Isis said.

One of the paramedics asked Isis her name.

"Michelle Carter," Isis lied Country looked at her like what the fuck but he followed alone.

They put Isis in the back of the ambulance and they drove her to Saint Bernard Hospital. Her blood pressure was high, she was dehydrated and three months pregnant. Isis couldn't believe what she just heard.

Country came out the waiting room and asked Isis what was wrong.

"My blood pressure is high and I'm dehydrated," Isis said. She didn't want to tell Country she was pregnant in fear of losing him.

Country took Isis back to the room to get some rest and his phone started going off. It was a private number. The caller on the other end said, "Go get your daughter from my sister. I don't want her no more," followed by silence.

"This bitch," Country said. He just wanted to get his kids and take Isis back to New Orleans.

chapter nineteen

Isis woke up in a cold sweat. She had a nightmare about her mom killing Country. She got up to get a drink of water and she saw Country sitting there in a daze. "Baby, are you alright?" Isis asked. Country didn't respond. She touched his shoulder and Country jumped up. "What the fuck, Isis? Don't fucking touch me. Ever since I met you, my life has been bullshit. I can't take any of this shit," Country yelled. He was very irritated from the call he got from Ki Ki earlier. Isis jumped in his face screaming, "What the fuck did you just say to me? Oh, you want to talk about problems? Nigga, guess what? I don't have a mama or a daddy. My mom hated me because I came from a nigga that took her pussy and dignity." Country was about to respond, but she cut him off.
"No wait, nigga. I'm not done. My fucking mom beat the shit out of me every day after I turned a certain age. I never knew what love felt like until I met you or so I thought. To top it off, I'm pregnant and my baby could be yo right-hand man, Smiley's baby. The nigga who raped me in the same house my mom faked her death in, or this baby could be yours, a nigga that don't give a fuck about nobody's feelings but his own." Isis grabbed her stuff and left. "Bye Country. Don't worry about me, I'll find my way back home."
Country ran after her. "Isis! Isis!" he yelled. Isis turned around. "What man? What the fuck do you want? You said all you wanted to say in the room, right?" Isis looked at Country with hate and confusion in her eyes.

"Please baby, just listen to me. Please don't leave me like this. I love you so much. I'm going through so much. This bitch just called me and told me that she didn't want Kionna and to go get her. I know that ain't shit compared to what you are going through, but just please come back in the room," Country begged.

"Nigga, are you done? I have a flight to catch."

Country grabbed Isis' arm. "Man, get back in the room, now!" Isis was shocked, but she liked Country's aggressiveness. Isis turned and went back into the room.

"Just because I'm going back in the room doesn't mean we're cool," Isis said to Country.

"Look Isis, I'm not trying to argue anymore. I just want to get my kids, make sure they're safe, so we can take them back home and figure things out. I want to take care of you and our baby. You need to lay low while I take care of everything else."

"Nigga, you got me so messed up right now. I'm not going to stop because I'm pregnant! I want that nigga just like you do, so with that being said, we're in this together pregnant or not."

Country stared at Isis for a long time. "Isis, you're very hard headed."

"I'm not hard headed. I'm just not about to sit around and watch shit go down." She sat on the edge of the bed still furious at Country. She turned to look at him and said, "Come here." Country walked towards Isis and sat down next to her. Isis started to talk.

"Country, I do not know what's going on. All I know is you just flipped out on me for nothing. I'm just sitting here trying to figure out what's wrong with you and instead of you talking to me; you go off. I know that I wasn't honest about being pregnant, but I was so scared to tell you because I don't know whose baby I'm carrying. I don't know how to deal with being pregnant. I'm not mother material and I know that I would hate this baby if I have it and it's not yours. I know that I will treat this baby just like my mom treated me, so I'm going through a lot. However, I'm still willing to sit here and help you. I don't want you to keep talking to me like any kind of way every time something goes wrong. You go crazy on me. Let's just lay down and sleep this off. In the morning, we will go get your kids and go back home. We will make sure they're straight and then come back here and finish this nigga."

Country didn't know what to say. He just looked at Isis and laid down. As soon as they fell asleep, there was a knock on the door.

Isis got up and nudged Country. "Babe, somebody is at the door." Isis and Country both got up. Isis stood behind Country as he peeped through the peephole. The hotel management and the police were on the other side.

Country whispered, "It's the police."

Bang! Bang! Bang!

Isis pushed Country away from the door as she swings the door open. "Hello, how can I help you?"

"Hello, we got a call reporting loud noise in this room," the hotel manager said.

Isis noticed the officer looking at her leg. She walked closer and said, "My man and I were having a small disagreement. If you know what I mean." The officer was flattered by Isis' beauty.

"Hold up let me get you something for your troubles," Isis said.

Isis ran back in the room, Country was behind the door watching Isis. She came back door, gave the officer and hotel management a hundred-dollar bill a piece.

"Thanks, ma'am, remember to keep it down," and they both walked off. Isis went back in the room and shut the door.

"I see you put spells on niggas," Country smirked.

"No, I just know how to get out of bullshit. As a matter of fact, let's go get your son." They both got dressed and headed to the hospital. Isis and Country got in the car, Country put in Lil Durk cd and played the song, "My Beyoncé" and they both were singing the song together. Isis pulled into the hospital, she pulled out her fake ID, and they walked to the front desk asked for Kevin Clark's room. The receptionist took their info down and gave them their visitor passes.

"Good thing y'all came, they were getting ready to put him in foster care," the receptionist stated.

"So, he's ok? Can he go home? Isis asked.

"Yes ma'am, he can. The nurses should be able to give you more information."

Country and Isis got on the elevator and went to the room where Lil Kevin was. When Country saw his son sitting on the hospital bed all alone, he felt so bad. Isis touched his shoulder. "Go in there, baby, and get him ready. I'll talk to the nurse."

When Lil Kevin noticed his daddy walking in the room, he jumped into his arms. Country held Lil Kevin tight. He noticed Lil Kevin's face was cut and that made him mad. Isis stopped watching Country and went to speak with the nurse.

"Hi, my name is Michelle Carter. I'm here to pick up my son, Kevin Clark."

"Thank God someone came to pick him up. We have his discharge papers ready, but first, you'll have to speak with the detective that's handling this case. Officer Benny, the parents of Kevin Clark are here."

Officer Benny walked over to Isis and shook her hand. "Hello, Ms.?"

"Ms. Carter, but you can call me Michelle," Isis lied.

Officer Benny looked at her as if he knew she was lying. He turned toward the room and seen both of his nephews. He shook his head, walked into the room after Isis and shut the door.

"Babe, Officer Benny is here."

Country looked up. "What's up Unc?"

Isis looked at both of them confused, but she continued to watch. Country noticed that his uncle was acting differently.

"What's up Unc?"

"Country, sit down. We need to talk."

"Nah, I'm cool. I don't need to sit down. Talk!" Country yelled.

Country knew it was about to be some bullshit, so he told Isis to take Lil Kevin in the lobby and get snacks.

Isis took Lil Kevin to the bathroom. "Hold this gun," she said. "Do you remember the people who held you hostage?"

Lil Kevin nodded his head and said, "Yea."

"Look, if they come in this bathroom, blow their brains out. I'm going to check on your dad."

"Okay," Lil Kevin said. Isis walked back to the room and eavesdropped outside the door. She heard Country say, "Damn Unc, why are you doing me like this man? Please Unc, tell me you're lying." Isis was ready for war. She stood there and listened some more.

"Ki Ki is ova there at the spot. She got Murder and Smiley there and she's holding them hostage. You pay us and they're yours." Isis stood there with her mouth open.

"How much, Unc?"

"Fifty-grand for both of us," Officer Benny said. Isis was startled when her phone rang. She looked at it was a text from Mama Karen.

Mama: Kill him. He's not my real brother no way.

Isis ran back to get Lil Kevin. She walked into the bathroom and she heard the gun click. "Lil Kevin, it's me. Don't shoot." He walked towards her handing her the gun. They leave the bathroom and she bumped right into Officer Benny.

"See you later, Isis," he said chuckling.

Isis went back in the room and Country was packing up Lil Kevin's stuff. "Come on Isis. Let's go."

Isis grabbed Country hand and said, "I got you." That made him feel much better. They walked out the hospital ready to face whatever.

chapter twenty

Cream came back from the mall with her arms filled with bags from
PINK, Forever 21, Victoria Secrets, and Foot Locker. Cream stopped at
the loud man's apartment, but before she could knock on the door, one
of her exes grabbed her.
"What's up, Cream? I see you giving my time to another nigga."
"Ghost, can you please leave me the fuck alone? It's been over between
us," Cream screamed and yanked her arm away from Ghost.
"Listen, bitch, you know too much and we've done too much dirt
together for it to just end. Who is that little pretty bitch you've been
hanging with?" Ghost asked. Cream stood there with the dumb face.
"Why you want to know?" Cream asked him. Ghost walked closer to
Cream. He was so close she smelled the liquor he had been drinking on
his breath. Ghost was very dark skinned, he wore all black, his dreads
were down his back with white tips, and his eyes were hazel brown.
Ghost was nothing to be played with; he was pure evil. He pulled his
Gun out and yanked Cream in the stairway. He pulled her clothes off
and stuck his dick in her pussy. Cream didn't try to fight, she knew if
she would've fought back that Ghost would've blown her brains out, so
she just let him continue to fuck her. When he was done, he busted all
over her clothes and whispered to her, "Your little friend is next."
"Please Ghost, don't hurt her. She's not like that," Cream pleaded.
"Bitch, I've been following her and she got more than you know, so
either you get some big money from that bitch or I'll kill you both."

Cream called Isis' phone and got no answer. She decided to send her a text instead.

Cream: *Isis call me ASAP*

Cream went to her apartment and took a bath. She called Isis again and still no answer. *She's probably having fun up there. I'll just wait until tomorrow to call her.*

Cream really liked Isis and didn't want to hurt her or see her hurt. If it would've been someone else, Cream would have taken that offer. However, she'd seen something different in Isis. Cream decided to stay home instead of going to work. She called the loud man to come bring her two dub sacks and a Swisher. He finally gets there and Cream invited him in. she was about to use this lil nigga to her advantage.

"Aye loud, you wanna match?" Cream asked.

"Yea maw," Loud replied.

"Okay, go sit on the couch, put *Friday* in or a porn."

They both laughed. "Girl stop playing with me, you're not ready for this young nigga."

"Roll dat weed up, man. I'm about to go to my room and grab something really quick."

"Aight shawty. Hurry up."

Cream went to her room and took off all her clothes. She put her silk pink robe on and grabbed her Patron. She walked back to her living room and Loud was sitting there watching a porn flick. Cream rubbed against him and said, "I see you choose wisely."

They sat there for about an hour drinking, smoking, and talking shit. They waited until all the Patron and loud were gone to go into Cream's room. She played Future's "Rich Sex" and she danced for him. Loud was loving that, he'd always admired Cream's body. Loud was six-foot-one with caramel skin, his teeth were perfect and white with nice juicy lips. Loud knew he wasn't supposed to be in Cream's apartment while his girlfriend was downstairs probably taking care of his kids, but he didn't care. He turned his phone off; he wanted Cream to have all his attention. When Cream was done dancing, she took off Loud's clothes and sucked his dick. She deep throated his dick until it disappeared into her mouth. Loud's dick was nice and long, just like she liked it with a curve.

She laid loud on her bed, put a condom on his dick, and rode him nice and slow. "Umm girl, you got some tight and good pussy." He grabbed her ass.

"You like it, huh?" Cream whispered in his ear then she started licking his neck.

"Yes girl, bounce on this dick maw." Cream started rotating her hips.

"Maw, I want you to be my girl," Loud said. Cream knew her sex game was crazy; she had bitches and niggas hooked.

"Tell me you'll do anything for me, daddy."

"Yea maw, I got you," Loud said.

Cream felt Loud's dick throbbing in her pussy. She bounced harder on his dick. "You promise you'll do anything for me, daddy?"

"Yea maw, whatever ya want." Cream jumped off his dick, took the condom off and proceeded to suck and swallow all his cum. Loud fell asleep. He just didn't know he was about to be Cream's next victim. Cream got up the next morning; she checked her phone first to see if she had any missing calls or text messages from Isis. *Still nothing*, she thought. Loud had left in the middle of the night, he put a thousand dollars on her pillow.

"Oh shit, this nigga must love the pussy," she said aloud. She called Isis and this time to her surprise, Isis picked up,

"Hey ma, what's up? You coming back today or what? We need to talk," Cream said.

"I'm not coming back today, but I'll be back in a few days. Why? What's up?" Isis replied. She didn't really want to talk to Cream, but she answered anyway because Cream had been blowing her up.

"Okay, when you do touch down text or call me. It's important," Cream said and then they hung up. Cream was startled by a knock at the door. She put on her long t-shirt and ran to the door.

"Who dat is?"

"Bitch, open da door!" It was Ghost. Cream was a little scared, but she flung the door open anyway.

"Did you talk to your friend? Ghost asked.

"Yea, I talked to her today," Cream answered, sounding cocky. "She'll be back tonight."

"Okay, bring that bitch to the warehouse. I want to taste that sweet pussy and I know you want to taste it too," Ghost said and walked out.

He just didn't know he was about to get a surprise that he'd never forget. Cream made sure he was gone and she sent a text to Loud.

Cream: *Come upstairs*

Let me clean up a little we made a mess last night, she thought. Ten minutes passed and still no response. "Damn, what's up with him?" Cream said to herself. She grabbed her phone and she sent him another text.

Cream: *Are you busy? I need you...*

Loud: *Sorry Maw, here I come.*

Cream tossed her phone on the couch and finished cleaning. She went to the kitchen to make breakfast. As she was cooking, she zoned out and began to reminisce on the relationship with Ghost. It was a lot of deep secrets shared between the two. *I remember one day I woke up and he had a lady and man lying in a pool of blood on my bathroom floor. I couldn't believe it. He made me help him cut the bodies up and throw them in our garbage disposal.*

I can remember while we were cutting up the lady's body that she had a dead baby in her stomach. Later on down the line, I found out he killed them because that was his wife and she was pregnant by the man. I've been fucked up bout that for years. I really hate him. When I moved here from Chicago he was the first nigga I met. He was a cool nigga, so I thought until he started beating my ass and raping me. He even made me fuck his female cousin, so tonight will be his last night on earth.

Knock - Knock

Cream jumped. "Shit! Who is it?"

"Loud! Who else would it be?"

Cream opened the door and let him in. She had tears coming down her face. "What's wrong?" Loud asked.

"He said he's going to kill me," Cream said in a shaky voice.

"Who said that?" Loud asked.

"My ex. He is still in love with me. He said he'd seen you coming out my apartment."

"What the fuck? Who is your ex?"

Cream looked up at him and said, "Ghost."

Loud walked over to her. "Did you just say Ghost?" Loud knew Ghost wasn't a joke in these streets. He knew if he wanted her dead because of him being in her house, he was going to kill him too.

Loud sat on the couch, put his head down and screamed, "Fuck!" Cream walked up to him and rubbed his head. "We can get him before he gets us," she said still crying. You would've thought she was a Grammy award winner the way she was putting on. Loud looked at her like she was crazy, but he knew that was the only way he'd live.

chapter twenty one

"Loud, I know how we can get him. He always spends his night in this warehouse uptown. All we have to do is go there and kill him," Cream detailed her plan.

"Whoa, you're trying to jump in head first. In this Cream, you gotta be careful fucking with this nigga," Loud said.

"Trust me; I got this Loud. I just need you to be with me because I can't take him out by myself." Loud wanted to say fuck it and walk away, but he knew he had to get that nigga before he got him.

Ghost was in the warehouse laying down. It was six in the evening and he just was trying to relax. He barely got up to do anything. This is where he spent most of his days. The warehouse was filled with trash and week old take out from different restaurants. Ghost decided to get up and take a couple shots of Hennessy before it was time for Cream to bring him Isis. Ghost had money, but he doesn't live like it. He would rather take from others and torture people.

Ghost walked over to the area where he kept all his guns and drugs. He grabbed his AK-47, snorted a line and took five shots of Hennessy. *Man, I'm feeling good*, he thought. Sitting back down he did another line and he started nodding off...

Click, Click, Click...

He heard something. He turned around, but no one was there. "What the fuck? I need to leave this shit alone." Ghost started to nod off again, and shortly he started hearing sounds again. He smacked himself. "What the fuck?"

113

Cream and Loud was just pulling up to the warehouse, it was just starting to get dark. Cream walked in first. She wore an all-black leather catsuit with a pair of knee-high leather boots. Her hair was in a long ponytail. Loud was right behind her. He was kind of nervous. *But it is what it is,* he thought.

"Stay here," Cream said. "When Ghost and I walk back this way, blow his brains out. Here's the gun. Cheer up, this will be easy." She kissed him on the jaw as she walked off. Loud didn't hear anything but her heels clicking on the floor.

Damn man, I should leave this bitch in here, Loud thought to himself. *How I know this bitch not lying about Ghost wanting me dead.* Loud was sweating and he was fidgeting. *I can't do this. I'm out.* As soon as he was about to leave, he heard a gunshot.

Cream walked into the area where Ghost normally would be. She was startled by what she just walked into. Reaching for her gun, she remembered leaving it with Loud. "No, shit, fuck! How am I gonna get out of this one?" She peeped in the room again, and there was a fragile woman searching around Ghost's things. She was moving shit around, crying and just going crazy.

Cream wanted to leave, but something wouldn't let her. She finally turned to the left side of her and she sees Ghost's body lying on the ground with multiple stab wounds and his throat was slashed. She also noticed the window was shot out. Ghost's gun was right by Cream's foot. Cream started laughing to herself. "This dumb ass nigga let this little ass woman kill him."

Cream wasn't scared just a little shocked. She walked in the room and the lady jumped. Cream walked towards her and the lady picked up a knife. "What you about to do with that knife? Put that shit down before I beat yo ass," Cream said.

"Back up!" the lady yelled. "I will kill you."

"Kill me for what? I hope you don't think I'm against you for murking this piece of shit ass nigga," Cream started laughing. "How did you do it and why?" she asked.

The lady started crying, "He killed my mom and he raped me. I couldn't let him get away with that. I'm still fucked up from the shit. This nigga is dirty. I watched him beat my mom for years. He used to smack me around. One day he came to our house high and drunk, when I was eleven years old. He came in, tied my mom up, duct taped her mouth shut, and made her watch him violate me. He rammed his dick in every spot that had a hole. I've been in and out of mental facilities because of this. When he was done fucking me, he took my mom out the house. I never knew where he was taking my mom until I woke up one morning and my aunt came in to tell me that they found my mom's body parts dismembered in a garbage disposal near our house. My mom was five months pregnant with my brother."

Cream's mouth dropped. "What was your mom's name?" Cream asked. "Gloria," the lady said. A tear fell down Cream's face; she couldn't believe what she was hearing. *If she was looking for Ghost I know she's probably looking for me. How the fuck did she know that he was in New Orleans?* Cream didn't waste any time, she grabbed the gun off the floor so quickly and blew the lady's head clean the fuck off. She turned around to leave and Loud was right there.

"What the fuck did you just do? Bitch, you're crazy. Let's get the fuck out of here before the police get here," Loud said while grabbing her arm.

Cream snatched away from him. She looked at him for a long time thinking to herself, *should I kill this nigga? How much did he hear? How long was he standing behind her? This nigga had better not try anything stupid.* "Hold up, Loud. Let me get this nigga's stash." Cream grabbed everything she could, she took the gun she used to kill Gloria's daughter, cleaned her fingerprints off, and sat the gun by Ghost making it look like he killed her.

chapter twenty two

Isis and Country went back to the room, grabbed all their stuff, and went to another hotel on the other side of town. They'd finally gotten Lil Kevin to go to bed. He was excited about being with his dad. *Lil Kevin was strong,* Isis thought. *I would've been somewhere curled under a rock.* Isis and Country sat on the couch watching TV. Country was the first one to fall asleep. Isis got up, grabbed her gun off the table, and made a phone call.

"Hey, is he still there?"

The caller said, "Yea." Isis hung up and left out the house.

Officer Benny was parked in front of Ki Ki's apartment waiting for her to come out. Kionna was in the back seat. "Uncle Benny, where are we going? I want my daddy."

"I'm about to take you to your daddy when your mama comes back down, baby. Sit back."

Isis pulled in the back of Officer Benny's car. She put the silencer on her gun, got out and walked towards his car. She tapped on his window. He looked up to see Isis and before he could say another word, she let out two shots. The glass shattered and she heard screams coming from the back seat. Isis looked in the back seat and to her surprise it was Kionna. Her first instinct was to grab her, run to her car, and drive as fast as possible.

Ki Ki came out the apartments just in time to catch a woman taking her baby. She didn't know this woman was Isis.

"Hey, give me my daughter!" Ki Ki screamed.

Isis turned around and blew Ki Ki a kiss and said, "You're next." Isis got into her car and sped off. Kionna was in the back-seat crying, so Isis turned around and said, "I'm about to take you to your daddy. Ok?" Kionna nodded her head and said yes.

Isis gets to the room as she opened the door to walk, she is surprised that Country was standing in the kitchen with his back turned towards the door. "So Isis, where have you been?"

"Daddy!" Kionna screamed, running from the door. Country turned around to see his daughter running to him.

He looks up at Isis, and then he grabs Kionna. He picked her up, kissing her. "Hey, daddy's baby. I missed you. Who do you love, Kionna?"

"You, daddy!" Kionna yelled so loud she woke up Lil Kevin. Kionna and Lil Kevin were very close. Lil Kevin was happy to see Kionna. He ran to her and gave her a big kiss on the jaw.

"I missed you, Kionna."

"I missed you too, brother."

Isis watched them with tears in her eyes. She walked into the room and laid down on the bed beginning to drift off into space. She thought about her mom. Every day she regretted killing her mom. *Mom, I miss you. I'm so sorry for what I did. Please forgive me.*

Country went in the room where Isis was, he had left Lil Kevin and Kionna in the other room to play. Isis was just dozing off when he entered.

"Hey." Country kicked the bed, and Isis jumped up.

"Yes, Country?"

"What did you do Isis?"

"I'm confused, Country. What do you mean what did I do? I went to get your daughter."

"Isis, you can't keep making moves without me, baby. You could've gotten hurt," Country said.

"I'm sorry, baby. Come here," Isis responded, looking sad. Country laid down next to Isis and she kissed him. They both held each other until they were both asleep.

Lil Kevin and Kionna were in the room talking. "My mom is dead. I think Isis is about to be my mom now," Lil Kevin said.

"I saw my mom and Uncle Benny kissing. She told me not to tell daddy," Kionna said. "I want to stay here with my daddy, mom doesn't feed me," Kionna said. "She just goes out with Uncle Benny."
"When I get grown, I'll always protect you, sis." They both hugged each other.
The next morning, Country was getting the kids ready to go back to New Orleans. Isis walked into the kitchen; she fixed the kids some cereal.
"Isis, come here when you're done," Country yelled.
"Okay. Lil Kevin and Kionna, come eat."
Isis went in the room with Country. "We're leaving today to take them to my mom," Country said.
"Ok, but-" Isis started to talk, but Country stopped her.
"Pack your stuff," he said. Isis was beginning to pack. "Oh yea, where was Kionna when you picked her up and don't lie?"
Isis stood there for a minute and as soon as she was about to open her mouth, Kionna ran into the room. "Daddy, we're done eating." Country already knew what happened because Kionna told him last night. He just wanted to see if Isis was going to keep it real with him. He was tired of his mom and Isis doing things on their own. That's why when he got back to New Orleans he was leaving her there.

chapter twenty three

They finally get to the airport. "Sorry Country," Isis said.
Country turned around. "For what?" he responded.
"You know, for what I did. I'm just so anxious to please you that I don't
think sometimes." Isis wanted to say your mama told me to do it, but
she knew it will cause more problems so she took the blame.
"What happened, Isis?"
"I shot your Uncle Benny. I didn't know Kionna was in the back seat
though. I'm so sorry I didn't know what they were going to do with her.
I heard what he was saying to you at the hospital and that pissed me
off."
"Isis, you have to let me be the man, baby. You have to know that I
know what I'm doing and if I lose you, I would lose my world."
Country grabbed and hugged her. "Plus, you're pregnant with my
baby." He touched her stomach and Isis jumped. She almost forgot she
had a baby growing inside her. They got on the plane and off they
went. Isis couldn't wait until this war was over so she could live a
normal life.
They finally made it home. Isis walked in first and Mama Karen was in
the kitchen cooking fried chicken, rice, sweet corn and butter biscuits.
"Hey kids, your Nana is in the kitchen." Mama was so busy cooking
and blasting Marvin Gaye's music, she didn't even hear them come in.
The kids ran into the kitchen screaming, "Nana!" Mama jumped with
tears in her eyes.

"Hey, babies!" She was confused. "Where's the other one?" She looked at Isis. *Mama better not fuck with me today. I don't care about her ass being affiliated with the Mob, I will treat her whole fucking life.* Isis walked off and she pulled her phone out to text Cream.

Isis: *Cream, what you doing?*

Cream: *Nothing, chilling. You back?*

Isis: *I am. Are you at home?*

Cream: *Yep*

Isis: *I'll be ova there later.*

Cream: *okay bet*

Country walked in the room. "Isis, what are you doing?"

"Nothing, why what's up?" she replies.

"I'm about to go to the store. Do you need me to bring something back?"

"No baby, I'm cool." As soon as Country left, Mama walked in the room.

"Where's my grandson, Ja'von, at Isis?"

Isis looked at Mama strangely. "I don't know."

"What you mean you don't know?" She walked up to Isis and Isis jumped up quickly in defense mode. *Shit, I can't take any chance with this lady*, she thought.

"You have to go back Isis or my grandbaby will get hurt."

"Mama, why are you telling me to do all this? Country needs to handle something. I can't take the stress anymore," Isis said aggressively.

"Please go back with him and get my grandson. Please, Isis."

Isis just looked at her and said, "Okay."

It seemed like I will never catch a break, she thought. She put on her shoes and went to Cream's house. As she was leaving, she told mama that she'd be back and she was going for a walk. Isis gets to Cream's house and the door was unlocked. "This bitch is always leaving her door open," Isis said. She walked in Cream's house. Cream and Loud was in there talking. Isis couldn't believe what she was hearing. She laughed to herself and said, "This bitch is crazy, man," as she walked back out the door. She didn't want Cream to know what she heard. Isis was in deep thought all the way back home.

I can't believe Cream did that for me. It has to be a reason why. Does she want something out the deal? Is she really trying to be a friend to me? I just know this bitch just killed two people in one day. I'm so ready to set up shop though. I'll text Cream later and let her know I got sick or something. I'll let her know that I want to put some dope out on the streets and I'll give her a brick or something.

Isis walked into the house and Country was sitting right in front of the door waiting on Isis. "Where you been?"

"I went walking at this park. Why?"

"I just wanted to know. I told you to be careful out here, Isis," Country said.

"Yeah, I know. I'm cool though."

"We're leaving in two days. I was about to leave your ass up here. It's a good thing you told me the truth."

Isis looked at that nigga as if he was crazy. "Boy, and I would've been right on the next flight."

"Mama, what are you doing?"

"Nothing baby, I'm just in here enjoying this time with my grandkids that's all." Isis walked into her room and picked up the diary to read it.

Dear Daughter,

I hope you're doing well and settled into the new home that I got for you. I hope you killed that nigga, Smiley. If not, get him and everybody he's affiliated with. Those niggas ain't shit. Be very careful with how you approach them, it could be your last day alive.

Ps: Don't get lazy

Isis instantly thought of Country. *Could he be just like Smiley? Does he really love me? Only time will tell.*

Mama, why are you doing this to me? My life will never be normal. All I want to do is party and go to school...

"Hey Isis, you want to eat?" Country called out to her.

"Country, no. Not right now, maybe later." *I wonder what Cream is doing let me text her crazy ass.*

Me: *Hey, I came up on a brick of coke. You want to open up shop with me?*

Cream: *Damn bitch, why you didn't come ova? And hell yea!*

Me: *Got sick I'll be there tomorrow.*

Cream: *Sick? Are you preggo, bitch?*

Isis let that last text play in her head.

Cream: *Are you preggo?*

Damn, a bitch really about to have a baby. I don't know who baby this is all I know is I don't want a fucking baby. Let me put my mom's diary up before mama finds it. She's been acting strange lately.

Kionna ran into the room. "I love you, Isis. Thanks for bringing me to my daddy."

"You're welcome, Kionna. Come give me a hug." Kionna ran to Isis. "Are you going to be my mommy too?"

"Yea baby, I will." *Damn, my life will never be normal. I guess I'll make the best of it,* Isis thought.

chapter twenty four

Damn, let me clean up before Isis comes today. I need to tell her everything about what happened. I hope she still fucks with me. Loud's ass has been tripping ever since he witnessed what I did. Shit, I told that nigga this is not my first murder and wasn't goin be my last. Where the fuck is my blunt at, damn? He probably smoked my shit. Today is gon' be a good day. Her phone started ringing and it was Ghost's sister. "Hello. Cream, have you heard from my brother? He was supposed to come to my baby's party the other day."

"Nope girl, you know me and Ghost had been broken up, but if I talk to him I'll let you know," Cream said, and then she hung up.

Isis went in her basement to get a brick for Cream. She wanted to see her work potential on the street. I'm not trying to be out there like that unless I have to, I'll let Cream handle pushing this shit. If she fucks up, that's on her. She'll never get anything else. Damn, it looks like somebody has been down here searching. Probably mama, she's becoming a pest, but I'll put up with it because of Country. I just want her to stop forcing so much shit on me. She reminds me of my mom in a way.

"Country, I'll be back. I'm about to go for a walk."

"You need me to go with you?"

"No, I'm cool." Isis left.

"Son, do you trust her?"

"Why you ask me that ma? Because she's going for a walk?" Country asked.

"It's something about Isis. She's not that sweet girl that left my house that day."

"Mom, you wouldn't be nice either if you been through what she's been through!"

"What do you mean Country? I've been through it all. You need to start putting your feet down with Isis before she leaves you for the world."

"Mama, you really think she's going to leave me?" Country asked.

"Yes, I do, especially since she's getting to know this wicked city."

Country just looked at his mama and walked off.

Isis finally got to Cream's house. This time she knocked on the door, giving Cream time to answer.

"Who is it?" Cream hollered through the door.

"It's me, Isis!"

Cream ran to the door to let Isis in and gave her a big hug. "I missed you, bitch. Sit down, I have so much to tell you." Cream's energy was through the roof. Cream told Isis everything including things about her past. Isis couldn't believe the shit Cream had been through in her life.

"Damn Cream, I would've never thought you grew up like that."

"It's cool, Isis. I will get through it all."

"Well here, take this. You can have it. This is going to be your meal ticket out the projects," Isis predicted.

Country was blowing up Isis' phone after his mom told him that he needed to watch her. Hours had passed and Isis was still gone.

Man, I need to tell Country that I have a friend out here. He might get mad, but who cares? I need a friend or two. My life is a hot mess right now.

Isis called Country back. "Hey babe, I just met this girl. Her name is Cream and she seems really cool. She was telling me about the city and I was so deep in our conversation that I didn't hear my phone."

"Isis, you're tripping ma. You need to get home now."

"Ok babe. I'm on my way," she said, ending the call with Country.

"Cream, I gotta go. My man is tripping again."

"Alright, luv. Call me tomorrow," Cream said.

When Isis got to the house, Mama was already on the porch. "Isis, where have you been?"

"I already told your son what was up. Can I leave to get a piece of mind?"

Mama looked at Isis and said, "New Orleans is not the city to be just walking around in. You gotta be careful; you're becoming a little stupid."

Isis got irritated and walked off, "Country had better get his crazy ass mama before I smack her. Her mouth is too slick for me. Country, where are you at?"

"I'm in here packing, we're leaving tonight. Something came up, so let's go. We need to get there before it's too late."

Damn, we finally made it to the airport. As soon as Isis got on the plane she puked up all of her guts on Country's Rock and Revival jeans. I don't think I will be able to carry this baby much longer. This Chicago air smells like piss and shit. The police were on every block. I'm ready to leave already. "Baby, I need to tell you something," Country interrupted her thoughts.

"Yes, Country?" Isis responded.

"Benny isn't dead."

"Oh fuck! What do you mean he isn't dead? I let my whole clip off in that nigga. This can't be true." Isis punched the seat.

"Calm down baby, I got this. My mans is on his way to the hospital to finish him off and we're about to go find Murder and Smiley."

"What about your baby momma?"

"I'll take care of that too."

"Ok baby," Isis said.

They pulled into this empty lot where they met the same man that came to New Orleans to drop off the heroin. He was also the same man that cleaned Isis' house after she murdered her mom and Lah Lah. He handed Country a key and Country handed him a white envelope, then they parted ways.

I wonder what the fuck this nigga got going on. That's why I like doing my own shit. I never want to walk in a situation blinded ever again, but I'll let him lead the way, she thought.

They pulled up in front of this house and Country told Isis, "Get out the car Isis. Let's go inside. Make sure you grab your gun."

Her blood instantly started rushing and her trigger finger started itching. She followed Country to the door; he put the key in and opened the door. The house was pitch black. Isis had her gun cocked and ready to blow. When they got to the back room the smell of old blood filled the air.

"You ready baby?" Country asked.

Isis nodded her head. "More ready than I'll ever be."

When they made it in the room, this bitch Ki Ki was hog-tied to bed ass hole naked. When she saw Isis' face, she tried to get loose but whoever tied this bitch to the bed made sure she wasn't going to escape.

"Wait, something isn't right," Country said.

"What do you mean baby?"

"Smiley and Murder were supposed to be here, not this bitch," Country explained.

chapter twenty five

Isis couldn't believe what she just heard. Smiley was supposed to be here.

"Hold my shit." She took off her coat and gave it to Country. Isis jumped on top of Ki Ki.

"Where the fuck them niggas at? You got your dumb ass in here tied the fuck up because you want to set your baby daddy up."

Isis pulled the tape off Ki Ki's mouth. "Arrrrgh!" Ki Ki screamed.

"Shut the fuck up, bitch." Isis punched Ki Ki in the mouth.

Ki Ki laughed. "My baby daddy, bitch? That's not my baby daddy. Officer Benny is the father of my child. Now take him his daughter because right now, bitch, I don't give a fuck if I live or die."

Isis was about to shoot Ki Ki, but Country grabbed her. "Stop Isis."

"You're a bogus ass bitch," Isis said.

"Let me up bitch, and let me up right now. I'll beat your ass hoe."

"So, Kionna is not my baby, Ki Ki? I really hope you're lying to me right now. You know how I feel about my first daughter. Please tell me you're lying, Ki Ki."

Ki Ki was silent. She really wished that she would have never said those words. Truth is Ki Ki loved Country. He was her first love, but he played her and fucked her head up. "Just kill me, Country. Take me out my misery," she begged.

"Nah bitch, that will be too easy," Isis said. "Where the fuck is Smiley at bitch?"

"Does it look like I know where they are? I'm in here."

"So, how you get here? They were supposed to be here," Country asked Ki Ki, but Ki Ki refused to answer.

"Baby, I don't know why you're wasting your time with this bitch. Shoot her."

"Shut up Isis!" Country yelled.

"Honestly, I don't know how I got here. Somebody put bag ova my head and brought me here. When I got here, I heard a lot of noise. Murder and Smiley were thanking some woman for bringing me to them. How this bitch knows about me or where Smiley was, I don't know. I don't know. I'm sorry, Country."

Isis pulled the trigger and blew Ki Ki's brains out.

"What the fuck Isis? Why you do that?" Country asked in disbelief.

"Because the bitch is lying. This is a fucking set up. Let's go." Isis got in the car and Country didn't say a word. He wanted to snap on Isis for being so hot-headed. Isis knew she fucked up; maybe Ki Ki had more to say. *Oh well, she's dead now,* Isis thought.

Country drove to the nearest gas station. he got out the car to make a phone call. "Mom, I think somebody is trying to set me up. This shit is crazy and Isis is so hot-headed. She just killed Ki Ki."

A smile crept across Mama's face. She was happy to hear that Isis was out there handling business.

Mama knew Country wasn't a killer. that's why she wanted to teach Isis everything she knew. She wanted Isis to be about that life. Mama knew she didn't have long to live due to a rare disease. Country didn't know that Mama was sick and how much she really wanted him to be with Isis, she just didn't like Isis doing her own thing in New Orleans.

"Look, I'm going to call one of my buddies to see if they can find out any info on Smiley. I'll call you back. Until then, go lay low for a couple hours."

Country hung up the phone. "Fuck that shit, man. I'm going to Smiley momma's house."

"Who the fuck is this nigga talking to, leaving me in the car and shit? I hope he's not mad at me. If he is, oh fucking well. I don't give any fucks. I didn't come out here to have a conversation, I came down here to kill these niggas," Isis spoke aloud. Country got back in the car; he slammed the door and sped off. "What's wrong with you?" Isis asked him. Country didn't say a word. "I guess you're mad at me because I killed your baby momma!" Before she knew it, Country hauled off and slapped the shit out her leaving Isis in shock.

"Shut the fuck up, Isis. Now!" Country pulled up in front of this raggedy ass building. He jumped out and left Isis in the car.

Isis sat there looking confused. She was just about to hop out the car when she saw a lady and a man walk into the building. *Fuck, fuck, fuck,* Isis thought. *Where is my phone? I need to call him ASAP. Fuck it I'm going in.* Isis jumped out the car that she left running just in case they need to make a run for it. The only thing she was thinking about was saving her man. She heard a lot of commotion inside the building, so she ran as fast as she could. Her stomach was hurting so bad, but she didn't care. All she wanted to do is get to Country.

"Where the fuck is Smiley?" Country yelled. He had the gun to Smiley's momma's head and Murder was standing there with his gun out. The only thing he can think about was Isis. *Man, I hope Smiley didn't grab Isis. What the fuck was I thinking leaving her down there?* His heart was pumping, his trigger finger itching. As soon as he was about to empty his clip, he heard a loud gunshot. He looked over to see Isis standing there with tears in her eyes. She had just shot Murder in the back. She locked eyes with the lady from the bank, Smiley's mom! Country dragged Smiley's momma to the car and put her in the trunk. They didn't know they were being watched.

I can't believe this bitch from the bank is Smiley's mom. That's why she was watching me like that. Did I look familiar to her? Country is a wreck right now, I'm just ready to kill again. What's happening to me? I have become a menace. "Country! Country! Are you ok?" Isis asked frantically.

"Yea ma, I'm cool. I can't believe what I'm about to get ready to do. I'm sorry for hitting you, Isis." he grabbed Isis' hand.

Isis was confused she didn't know what Country was about to do, but she was willing to ride with her man. They pulled up to Lake Michigan, took Smiley's momma out the trunk and as soon as Country was about to kill her a car pulled up.

"Freeze bitch!" Officer Benny hoped out the car. When Isis saw the person on the passenger side, her heart stopped.

Country looked at Isis and said, "Game time!"

Officer Benny had Country's other son, Ja'von, in the car with him and that bitch ass nigga that dropped the drugs off at the house.

I can't believe this shit. Why is it that everybody we run with is crooked? I don't know how Country and I are gonna get out of this, but something got to shake, she thought.

"Bitch, you thought you can shoot me and get away with it?" Officer Benny said as he pointed his gun towards Isis. Smiley's momma was laying in the sand crying for dear life.

"I wish this bitch will shut the fuck up before I slice her fucking throat." Country was just standing looking stunned. "I'm not really worried about shit and I'm not afraid to die."

Bang! Bang! Bang!

Shots were fired. Country had pulled a fast one and shot Officer Benny in the face. His body dropped to the ground. Isis walked over to the Cleanup guy when he starts pleading his case. "Please, Country. Man, don't kill me. Your mama sent me here to save you."

Isis new he was lying, but before she could pull the trigger, Ja'von had already put one in his dome.

Country always knew his son was a savage. Tasha would always let him be out thugging with the big guys, so it didn't shock him one bit that his son had killed the cleanup guy.

"Oh, my goodness. What the fuck did he just do?" Isis walked over to Ja'von and tried to take the gun.

"Bitch, don't touch me. You're not my momma."

Isis turned and looked at Country. Country nodded his head, giving her permission. Isis turned back to Ja'von and said, "Give me the gun, lil boy." She snatched the gun from him and walked towards Country.

"Please kill this crying bitch."

Country pointed his gun at Smiley's mom and put a bullet in her head. He and Isis tossed her body in the lake.

***

Smiley had just walked back in his mom apartment and the first thing he saw was Murder stretched out on the floor gasping for air.

"What the fuck happened to you, man? Where's my momma?"

"Country and his bitch took her…"

chapter twenty six

Cream was back at home living the good life. She couldn't get in contact with Isis and had been calling her all week.

"Damn, I can't believe I made fifty-grand already."

Ever since they found Ghost's body I've been getting a lot of heat, so I moved. They think I stole his drugs and money not knowing my friend plugged me. This nigga, Loud, is still scared talking about the police is looking for him. I told that nigga why would the police be looking for you and you ain't do shit. I'm not worried about shit; I'm living right now. On top of that, some old ass lady keeps coming around telling me to stay away from Isis. I can't wait to talk to her because that lady is tripping she's been threatening me and everything. I don't know what my girl Isis is into, but I'm ready to ride. Therefore, if that old bitch comes around again, I'm going to send her to God...

"Man, it feels so good to be in this big house by myself. It's better than that small ass apartment that I was in just a short time ago. I miss my friend Tati. I wish that she could-" Cream was interrupted by her phone ringing and it was Isis calling.

"Hello," she answered.

"Hey, girl! What's up? You've been calling me?" Isis said.

"Yeah bitch, it's going down up here. Bitch, the money is on deck," Cream excitedly replied.

"Oh, yea? That's what's up. I'll be back up there in a few days."

"Isis, why do you sound tired?" Cream asked.

"Cause I am, Cream."

"Okay, one more thing before you go. Some old lady has been coming around here threatening me about hanging with you. Is it something I need to know or do?" Cream asked.

"Naw, I got it. Cream, thanks for everything. I'll talk to you later," Isis rushed her off the phone.

Isis couldn't believe Mama was snooping around in her business again. "This lady is really crazy. I need to check her ass in a nice friendly way. I'm tired of everything. Right now, it feels like we will never catch Smiley and I heard Murder didn't die. Not only that, this baby in my stomach got me fucked up!" Isis fussed.

Country came walking into the room asking, "Baby, you hungry?" Isis just looked at him like he was crazy. She didn't know what it was, but she was starting not to like Country. *I think I'm going to run off.*

"Yeah, can you go get me an Italian beef deep with cheese? Make sure it's well deep with mild peppers on the side," Isis said.

"My baby got you eating huh?" Country smiled.

"Country, if you say so!"

Country knew something was bothering Isis and he really couldn't pinpoint what it was exactly. He knew her emotions were getting the best of her or maybe she's tired of this lifestyle. "I need to make sure Isis is ok because right now it looks like she's losing it," Country vowed.

"Okay baby, I'll be back in a little bit," Country said while walking out the door.

Isis instantly started packing up her stuff, getting ready to leave.

"Man, I'm tripping. I don't think I need to go anywhere. What the fuck am I thinking? I can't leave Country hanging, he's all I got." Isis felt nauseated, so she ran to the bathroom and threw up a lot of clear liquid. Her head started spinning.

"I can't take this anymore. I'm sick as hell, my head hurts… This baby got to go."

Ja'von walked up to her. "Aye, you straight?"

"Yea I'm cool, just a little sick."

"How many months are you?" Ja'von asked.

"Ja'von, what are you talking about?"

"Your stomach; it looks like how my momma's stomach looked. She's pregnant by my daddy too."

Damn, that's crazy. He doesn't even know his momma is dead and I didn't know Tasha was pregnant. But by who?

"Ja'von, who was you with all this time?"

"I was with the lady y'all killed at the lake. I'm glad that bitch is dead. My momma dropped me off to her and I ain't seen her since."

"Watch yo mouth!" Isis said while looking at Ja'von. She was amazed at how much he looked and acted just like Country. "Ja'von, why are you happy that she's dead?"

"Because she was-" Country walked in and Ja'von became quiet. He walked off from Isis.

"Why y'all get quiet when I walked in? What's going on?" Country questioned.

"Nothing," Isis lied. "I just got really sick and Ja'von came in here to check on me. Where's my food? I'm hungry." Country handed her the food.

"Aye, we got moves to make, so you gotta make this fast. Ja'von, you're going to have to get on the plane by yourself, Isis and I have some unfinished business to handle."

"Dad, can I stay here with y'all? I can stay in the room. I don't want to get on the plane by myself."

"I'll think about it, Ja'von. Go sit down I need to talk to Isis."

"Isis, have you ever met your pops?" Isis was looking at Country like he was crazy.

"No, why you ask me that?"

"Because my mom just told me some weird ass shit. You might want to sit down for this," he started to explain.

"No, I'm good standing up. Just tell me."

"So you remember John who delivered the package to our house, the cleanup guy, the one who was just with Benny?"

"Yes."

"That was your daddy."

"Wait, what? Come again. Now, I gotta sit down. I can't believe what you're saying to me right now." Isis held her head down and started to cry. "Country, I can't believe this. Please tell me you're lying right now."

"Baby, there's more. Tamika wasn't your real mom! She stole you from your real mom."

I can't believe what he's saying. Is it true that my mom isn't my mom, but what about the diary? "Where's is my real mom? I know one thing; I can't take this on top of all this other shit."

"Isis, there's more," Country said. He put his head down.

"John had been watching you for a long time. He didn't want your mom, I mean Tamika, to know that he knew where y'all were living," Country went on.

"She told me that she was raped," Isis uttered in disbelief.

"I met John through my mom. He's been our clean-up guy for years. He and my mom used to fuck around back in the day."

"Please don't tell me your mom is really my mom," Isis cried.

"Nope, but she knows who your mom is. You have a sister, a brother and a lot of cousins."

Isis couldn't stop crying. "That's why it's always been me and her! This bitch treated me like shit all my life." Isis started to think all the way back and it all started to make sense.

chapter twenty seven

"I need to go. I have to find her, Country. I think I remember who my mom is. This lady used to always come over and my mom, I mean Tamika, was so mean to her. She would bring two kids with her a boy and a girl. She told me that was her sister that she hated and then we moved away," Isis revealed. "Now that I think about it, my sister looks just like me and my brother looks like the cleanup guy."

"Isis, are you sure about this? I don't think you should go right now. Let's handle one thing at a time, do research, and then make moves. Don't forget we still gotta kill Smiley."

"Country, at this point I don't give a fuck about Smiley. You just put too much on me at one time and to expect me to just walk away and not think about this shit is dead wrong. Besides, can I believe your mama right now? How I know she's not a motherfucking lie and had been working with Tamika since day one? How do I know if I can trust you?" Isis started to get worked up. "She's been stalking my friend, Cream. Threatening her, telling her to leave me alone and stay away from me. What the fuck is that about?"

"Baby, my mom does a lot of crazy shit, but she will not do anything like that. Call her and ask her. Call her now."

Isis tried calling Mama, but there was no answer.

"She's not answering Country. It's always something. I have no luck. Ever since I've been on earth my life has been nothing but hurt and pain. Country, I need to go for a walk. This is too much for me."

"Hey Isis, can I go with you?" Ja'von asked.

Isis was going to say no, but she remembered that they needed to finish their talk.

"Come on lil boy."

Isis lit up her blunt and let the cool breeze smack her in the face. "Man, this air feels so good to me. I can't believe the world is so beautiful. Despite my fucked-up life, it is more out here."

"Aye Isis, the lady y'all killed used to kiss me and put her mouth on my private spot. She made me have sex with her in front of her friends. Sometimes they would all take turns," Ja'von opened up to her. "She even stuck a needle in my arm. She said it was to numb the pain for whatever they were sticking up my butt. Isis, I want to die sometimes, especially when I get sick for no reason. On top of that, my mom left me. Isis, why would she do that to me? I feel like everybody hates me including my dad," Ja'von cried.

Isis cried on the inside, but she had to keep a straight face. She needed Ja'von to stay tough.

"Ja'von, I'm sorry you had to go through this shit. It seems like we've almost gone through the same shit. We're gon get through this shit and we're gon kill everybody that stands in our way."

Isis phone started to ring and it was Mama calling her back.

"Hello, Mama." Isis rolled her eyes.

"Isis, Country told me what your friend said. I just want to let you know that it wasn't me. I've been in the house with my grandkids since y'all left. Isis, this is why I kept telling you to listen and stop moving so fast. She knows where you at now."

"Who knows where I'm at?" Isis asked.

" Your mom, Lovely. That's your real mom."

"Okay so, why would that be a problem that she's looking for me?" Isis questioned.

"Isis, she doesn't want anybody to know about you, especially since your sister and brother don't know. She might be trying to hurt you or get to you before you find them."

"Mama, that doesn't make any sense. Why wouldn't she want to see me if Tamika stole me from her?"

"Isis, it gets deeper than that. Trust me, if you can't trust anybody else. You might want to listen to me on this phone. Today, things may get easier or it may get harder, but please don't go into this alone."

Samantha Holt

"Fuck all this shit," Isis said while hanging up the phone. "I'm about to go kill Smiley. I'm tired of waiting around. I'll kill his ass and go back to New Orleans. Ain't no stopping me now. Come on, Ja'von. Let's go." *I know she didn't just hang up on me. I don't know about Isis sometimes. She just doesn't listen. I don't know why she feels like I may be against her, but I'm only trying to protect her and my son. I've been in this street life forever and I know things that nobody else knows. When I'd first seen Isis, I knew who her mama and daddy were. I even knew about that crazy ass bitch, Tamika.*

Isis is the middle child of her siblings; she and her brother had the same father, which was John. Lovely took John from Tamika and got pregnant with Isis. Tamika had lost her baby around that time, as she had delivered a stillborn. This is where the beef started. Tamika had taken Isis at the age of five from a park around the way. Lovely was devastated she was trying to get Isis back but no matter how much she tried Tamika crazy ass will threaten her. Lovely got tired of fighting Tamika, especially after she had gotten pregnant with her son.

Now since Lovely got her life together and married somebody else, word on the street is she looking for Isis, her sister, and brother to kill them. She feels as though her new life is a perfect picture and no one knows about her past.

Isis is being so hard headed and if she doesn't think, she's going to get all of us hurt. Lovely's ass is just as crazy as Tamika was. Two peas in the motherfucking pod.

I know I can stop this because Lovely wouldn't fuck with me. I know all her secrets.

"I don't know where this girl took my son and she's not answering her phone. I should have never told her shit about what Mama told me," Country fussed. "Every time I put her up on game this is what happens. She runs off, but this time she got my son with her. This girl doesn't care about anybody but herself. She will never care about my kids or me as I care about her. I'm tired of calling and she doesn't answer the phone."

Country heard someone knocking on the room's door. When he opened it to his surprise it was Isis standing there crying with a gun in her hand and Ja'von was gone.

"Isis where is my son?"

She was standing there crying not saying a word.

140

"Isis snap out of it where's Ja'von?"

"I'm so sorry Country for not answering the phone. I went to go and try to find Smiley and I was able to locate him. When I was about to kill him, Ja'von stopped me and told me not to do it. Seeing him brought back so many memories. I just want him dead."

"Isis, where's Ja'von?" Country asked again.

I sent him home on the plane. He's been through so much already. I didn't want him to see anything else that would traumatize him. I don't want him to end up like me, Country!"

"Isis, I understand. You want to make moves on your own, but you have to slow down baby. I'm trying not to give up on you, but you're not leaving me any more options."

"I'm sorry, baby. I'll do better this time. I promise."

"You might not like this, but we need to go back to New Orleans for a while. Look at us, baby. Let's clean ourselves up and you're pregnant, we need to check on the baby to make sure he or she is okay."

Isis didn't want to hear that, but she knew he was right. It was time to chill for a while, so she agreed.

"Okay baby, you're right."

What they didn't know was going back to New Orleans; they had more in store for them. Let the games begin.

chapter twenty eight

"Mama, we're back."

"Babe, that plane made me sick." They noticed that the house was quiet as hell.

"What the fuck?" I pulled my gun out and I started checking rooms. Isis got so nervous, Country was right behind her and they started hearing the kids screaming, "Daddy!" They put the guns away when they saw the kids were in the enclosed pool area swimming.

Mama reached out and gave Isis a hug. It kind of threw her off, but she hugged her crazy ass back.

"Ja'von told me you were pregnant. Now that I'm looking at you, girl, look at that belly! You look about six months," Mama exclaimed.

"I probably am now, mama," Isis said sounding off.

"What's wrong, you not happy?"

"Not really. It's too much for me. You know?"

"Yea, but we are going to get through this together. You just gotta stay comfortable okay," mama advised Isis.

"Yes, ma'am. I'll try. I'm tired now. I'm about to go lay down for a while."

Isis felt awkward talking to mama and mama felt awkward talking to Isis, but she told Country since Isis is pregnant she was going to help her out while respecting their house and space.

Where is that diary? Isis thought.

Dear Daughter,

If you're still reading this I'm probably long gone. I hope your life is moving along. I hope you're doing well, but I have another mission for you. Go into the den and get that chest, it has all my secrets in it.
What the fuck! I hope it got some shit in there about my real mom!
"I have to go back to my house; Country is going to be mad. This time I'll take Cream with me. I don't know if I want to leave though without letting him know. Man, we just talked about this shit. Maybe I can leave when I have this baby, but I need to know about these secrets she's talking about," Isis spoke aloud.
"Mommy!" Kionna came running up to me.
"Yes, baby?"
"I love you."
"I love you too, baby. Come give me a hug!" Isis loved all over Kionna.
"Okay. I can't wait until you have my sister. I'm ready to play house with her and comb her hair. Isis, I mean mommy, I want to stay here with you forever."
"Aww get up here. Kionna, you can stay as long as you want, baby. Come up here with me and take a nap. I'm tired and need you to hold me." Isis and Kionna stayed sleep until the next day. They were both woken up with breakfast in bed.
"Hey, my favorite girls in the world. Y'all slept good?" Country asked, kissing them on the forehead.
"Yes, we did," Isis beamed.
"Here, I made y'all breakfast."
"Aw thank you, baby. We appreciate it. Don't we, Kionna?"
"Yes, daddy."
"Isis, when you're done I want to go for a walk. Okay?" Country asked. Isis finished eating her food, got dressed, and went for a walk with Country.
The sun is shining, the breeze felt so good hitting her body on this Sunday afternoon. They were walking down the canal and Isis could feel somebody watching her. All of a sudden, she felt a sharp pain in her stomach. "Arrrrgh, Country my stomach hurts."
"Do you want to go to the hospital?"
"No! Just take me to the house. I probably need to lay down," Isis assumed.

The whole night the pain in her stomach had begun to get intense. She was tossing, turning, sweating, crying, and everything else. Those pains were very unbearable.

"Isis, get up. I'm taking you to the hospital. I think you're in labor."

"Country, I'm scared to go to the hospital. What's going to happen to my baby? I don't even know if my baby is okay and I know I'm not nine months already."

"Come on Isis, now."

They finally got to the hospital and situated in a room. The doctor told them that Isis was seven months pregnant and it was time for her to have the baby. He also said that the baby might not make it because he or she will be premature. They gave her some pain medicine and they induced her. Isis was so scared, but at the same time, she was ready. Her contractions were coming one minute apart and it was time for her to push. She gave the doctor maybe three good pushes and heard the doctor yell out, "it's a girl!" and then heard the baby crying. Isis just wanted to hold her and see who she looked like. They brought the baby to her and she was so small. It was hard to see who she looked like. She was so small. "God, please let her make it. I know I said I wasn't ready, but looking at her is making my heart melt. I can't stop crying. My heart is so heavy right now," Isis prayed. Country walked up and he was looking more hurt than Isis was.

"What's wrong babe? Are you okay?" Isis asked.

"No baby, I'm just hoping and praying she's ok."

"But babe what about the DNA test?" Isis asked.

I'm not worried about that test, baby. I Love you and want to make you my wife one day. We are going to get through all of this together. She's beautiful and I know she's mine. She's going to be strong just like her mom."

Isis couldn't stop crying. Country gave her a kiss and wiped her tears away.

The doctor came back in the room. "Mom and Dad, it looks like everything is fine with the baby. We will have to monitor her for a few weeks, so she will have to stay in the hospital."

Here come the tears again. "I can't believe what I've done to my baby. It's all my fault," Isis cried.

"Ma'am, everything will be okay. You're not the only mom that has delivered a premature baby," the doctor attempted to comfort her.

"I just feel like a failure."

"Don't! Things like this happen all the time. Have you figured out a name for the baby yet?" he asked.

"Yes, Miracle Nevaeh Johnson," Isis declared.

Country couldn't stop smiling. He was so happy that Isis gave the baby his last name.

"I'm so ready to go home. I've been in this hospital for three days now. I wish my baby can leave with me today because this is too much, and I'm still thinking about everything else going on in my life. I'm more stressed than anything. When I leave this hospital, I'll be telling Country that I need to go back to my house to pick some things up."

Mama came up to the hospital to see Isis and baby Miracle. She brought flowers and a card. They talked for a long time and Isis finally got Country to take the paternity test. She needed closure. The results would be coming in the mail in a few weeks and she was ready to let all this stress go before the baby comes home. After Isis kills a couple of niggas, then she'd be able to change around her life.

Cream came up the hospital to see Isis and she was mad because she didn't tell her she was pregnant. *This bitch had built us an Empire y'all.* Isis couldn't wait to get into this drug game, Cream made a million dollars already. She was able to give Isis half of it. *I'm glad I gave her a chance at friendship she has proven her loyalty to me.*

Cream finally ran into mama and she said that's not the same lady that's been coming at her about Isis. She told her that the lady's name was Lovely. And who is Lovely? My fucking real mama…

chapter twenty nine

I can't believe my mom is up here. Smoke must have told her where I was going. This bitch is crazy. Why is she at the police station? Nicole and Red came walking out of the station. Nicole looked like she was pissed at Red. She was treating the shit out of Red. If Keisha didn't know any better, she would've thought she was going to beat the shit out of Red. They finally got in the car everybody was quiet. Keisha broke the silence.

"Did y'all see that lady that walked out the police station?"

"No, I didn't see anybody," Nicole said.

"Yeah, you're talking about that lady that was in that nice ass gear, looking like money?" Red said.

"That was my mama. I know for a fact that she's looking for me."

"Bitch, you're tripping. She was asking the police about some bitch named Isis."

"Isis, why does that name sound so fucking familiar? Isis... Keep that name as a memo. I guess she's looking for the both of us."

"Bitch, are you sure that was your mama?" Nicole asked.

"Nicole yea, she had her name on her plates in big bold letters. LOVELY. I need to see who the fuck is this Isis person. I know if my mama is looking for her it gotta be some deep shit. My mama ain't wasting her time just looking for people it gotta be something. I need to call Smoke and let him know that I'll be out here for a minute. He probably wants to come out here."

Smoke was on the other side of town getting ready to have some bitches get at Re Re. She had her brothers run in his spot the other day.

It's a good thing he wasn't in there because if he was, he would've been a dead man.

"Aye hold on, my bitch is calling. What's up, ma?" Smoke spoke into the phone.

"Hey daddy, I was calling because I'm going to have to stay down here for a while. My mama has been looking for me and she's down here today looking for another girl, so I gotta see what's up with that," Keisha explained.

"Shit, that's cool too, ma. Maybe I can come down there. My cousin Country stays that way with his girl and kids. Maybe we can chill out there for a little while."

"Yes, baby that will be fine because Nicole is going to Atlanta to see her mama and Red's going to get her family to head back down here to stay. So, if you can, please come today."

"Okay, I'm about to call my cousin and tell him you're coming over. I'm getting on the next plane out."

"Okay, daddy. I can't wait. Text me their address." Keisha ended their call.

"Yep, bye."

"Okay y'all, I'm staying. Smoke is coming out here tonight and I'm going to his cousin's house until he gets here," Keisha explained to Red and Nicole.

"Bitch, are you sure? I mean if you want us to stay, we can."

"No, I'm straight. Y'all go have fun. I'm cool. I got some shit I need to take care of and it's personal now. He just texted me the address, turn up this block right here, keep straight and when you get to the corner, make a right. You're gon' see a big ass mansion."

"Damn bitch, me and my kids can come stay over here in this big bitch," Red said in awe.

They all started laughing. "I'm going to miss y'all so much. Give me a hug and light that blunt. Let's smoke before I go up in here. I don't know these people, might as well go in there high as hell, bitch," Keisha laughed.

Smoke texted her and asked her was she there yet, so she texted him back.

Me: Yeah baby, I'm here. I'm outside smoking before I go in.

Smoke: Okay. They're waiting on you. I'll be there in a few hours and his girl is there. She just resting, she just had her baby. Maybe y'all can get to know each other.

Me: I don't know about all that, but okay. I'm going in now, babe.

"I love y'all. I'll see y'all hoes later," she told Nicole and Red as she climbed out of the car.

Keisha walked up the stairs. She felt so uneasy like she was being watched. Damn, I'm tweaking hard as hell. I know she didn't follow me all the way to this rich ass neighborhood. Before she could ring the doorbell, some dude had let her in the house. If I didn't know any better, I would've thought this was Smoke standing in front of me. Damn, they look just alike.

"What's up lil lady? I'm Country, Smoke's lil Cousin."

"Hey what's up Country? I'm Keisha. It's nice to meet you."

"Come in, Smoke should be here in an hour or so. You can make yourself at home. Everything in here is available to you. I'm going upstairs to check on my girl. She just had our baby and our baby had to stay in the hospital, so she's feeling kind of down. Maybe she will come say hi to you later."

"Okay, no big deal I understand."

Country went back upstairs with Isis. Keisha was sitting in the living room when she heard footsteps behind her. The first thing she did was reach for her gun, but she thought against it. She heard a lady's voice say, "Isis." When Keisha turned around, she saw her mama standing in front of her. They both pulled their guns out.

Mama K had just walked in and she couldn't believe her eyes. It was Lovely and her daughter, Keisha, Isis' sister. Keisha and Lovely were ready to go to war, but when Lovely saw Mama K, she put her gun down.

"So, we meet again, Lovely. I thought you would be dead by now. Did you come here to kill your daughter, Isis?" Keisha's whole face dropped.

"What do you mean her daughter, Isis? Lovely, you got another daughter and her name is Isis? Are you trying to kill her too?" Keisha fired off questions back to back.

Isis was standing in the kitchen. She couldn't believe her ears or her eyes. Country had talked her into going downstairs to meet Keisha. She didn't know what she was walking into. All she knew was all these bitches had her fucked up and need to start explaining before she killed them all.

epilogue

Keisha & Isis Reloaded!

I know y'all probably like this crazy bitch Isis about to kill everybody including her sister, Keisha. Look, maybe I'll give her a chance, but my mama, Lovely, has to go. Shit, Country's mama too. She knows something. As a matter of fact, she knows way too much. See it was more to my Aunt Tamika's diary and I don't blame her for taking me from Lovely. While I was resting up, getting ready for my baby to come home, it gave me time to think and read.

I can't wait to see Smiley's bitch ass. He gotta die for all he'd put Tamika through. I know y'all like, wait she did you wrong, but I don't give a fuck. The shit is real. What he did to her the shit is beyond bogus. Shit, what everybody did to her was bogus. I'm about to tell y'all everything before I slaughter these bitches right where they stand.

Mama K is a part of the mob. The same mob that sent Smiley to rape Tamika, yeah, he raped her too. Mama K didn't like Tamika because Tamika had fucked Country's daddy. Wait, there's more. Tamika took me from Lovely because Lovely fucked John, my daddy, which was Tamika's man first. I know crazy right.

Now, I don't know if I want to kill my sister because she is as lost as I am, but if she jumps then I will blow her brains out on the marble floor she's standing on. I know my baby needs me, but somebody gotta dies up in this house tonight. I can't stand a snake ass bitch. Mama K knew she didn't like me from the jump. I honestly think she sent Smiley to rape me just like she did my Aunt T.

Country knew Tamika because she fucked his daddy. I guess that's what she needed to tell me about him until I killed her. Other than that, he knew nothing. He didn't even know that his mama and Smiley had ties.

I came from out the kitchen with my nine-millimeter cocked and ready to blow. As soon as I was about to shoot, Keisha shot Lovely and Mama K. She grabbed me and we got the fuck out of there. Why is she protecting me? Plus, she didn't even kill their asses?

"Wait, I gotta go back!" I screamed.

"Look, you need to stay right here. We're not thinking clearly!" Keisha yelled.

"Fuck all that bitch. I don't know you like that!"

"I know you don't, but bitch, I'm yo sister and right now you need to chill. Look at us. We look just alike bitch. Please calm down. We need to go somewhere so we can sort this shit out. We can kill them later," she tried to grab control of the situation.

I had to sit back and think. And you know what? This bitch is right, but how do I know I can trust her. I know she's my sister and all, but how do I know she's on my side.

"Keisha, let me see your phone so I can call my friend, Cream. We can go to her house!"

Cream's phone kept ringing. She finally answered.

"Hey, where are you at?" Isis asked.

"I'm at home," Cream said.

"Okay, I'll be there in ten minutes." When we got there, Cream was waiting outside. When we got closer to Cream, she couldn't believe her eyes.

"What the fuck, Isis? Who is this, your twin? Bitch, you gotta stop keeping secrets from me."

"Cream, don't start this shit. I just figured this shit out myself. I didn't know about Keisha until today. Bitch, it's some crazy shit going on, G. I need to leave New Orleans for a while. I got a lot of people to knock off the map."

"You need to think we're rich? Now, you have a daughter. We can get somebody to kill muthafuckas for you. Isis, you need to chill on the gunplay."

"I'm tired of people telling me to chill, but ain't nobody else chilling."

Keisha was looking at me like I was crazy. "What the fuck are you looking at me like that for?"

"You act just like me when I get mad. I don't want to listen to anybody. You think you know everything. You need to chill and chill now," Keisha tried to school me.

"I can't face Country right now. I'm pissed that I gotta vanish for a while. He can take care of Miracle. I'm on a mission until they're all dead, including his Mama."

I looked at Keisha and asked, "Are you ready?"

CPSIA information can be obtained
at www.ICGtesting.com
Printed in the USA
LVHW081710120419
613992LV00015B/259/P